A LOOK INTO
Indian Art
Cambodian Art

Conceived, Designed, and Illustrated by:
Mrinal Mitra

Series edited by:
Swarna Mitra & **Malika Mitra**

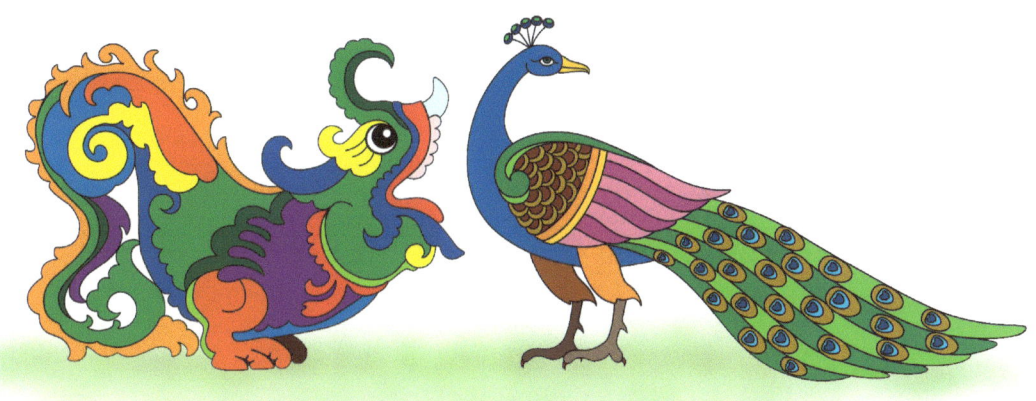

This series is dedicated to the citizens of the world;
from the young blooming minds of children, to the aspired individuals of all ages.

THE WORLD CULTURE ART
VOLUME-4

A LOOK INTO
indian art

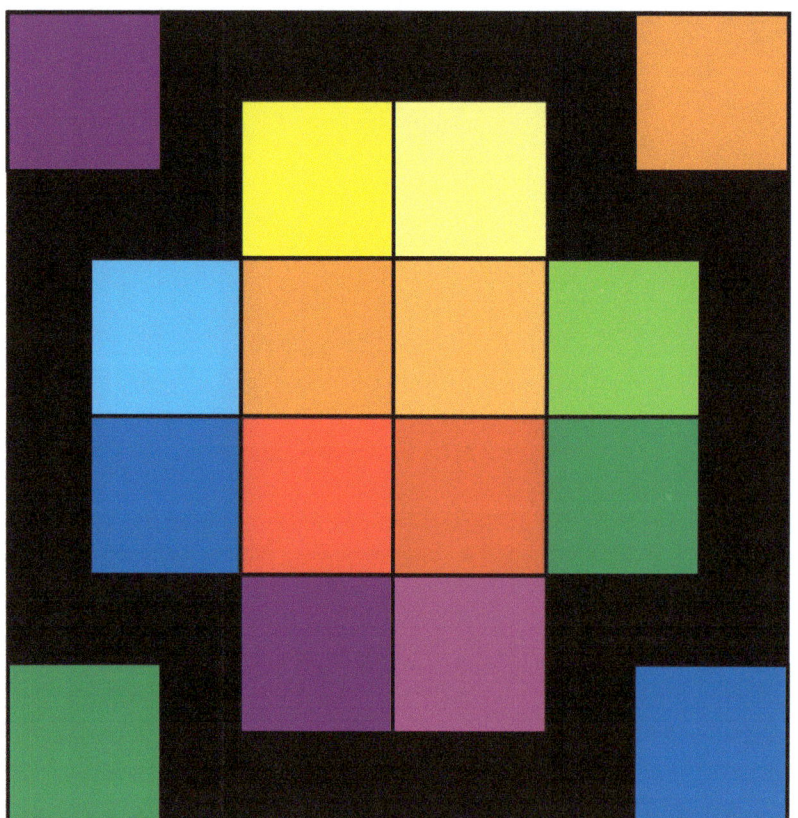

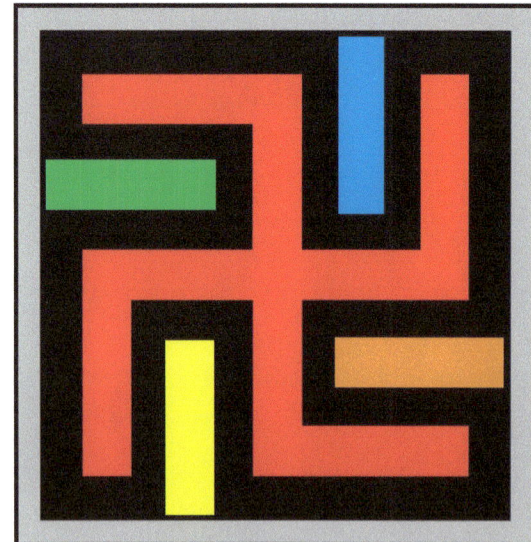
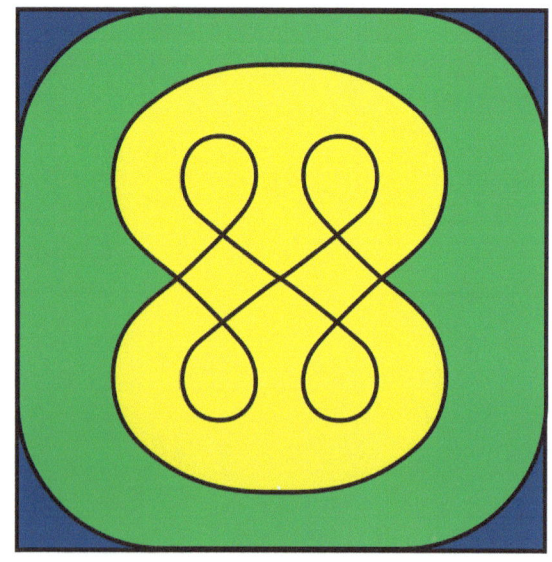

Seals found at Mohanjo-Daro, in the Harappan Civilization, depicting the Multiple Cross, Endless Knot, and Swastika. Over 5000 years ago.

Indian Art

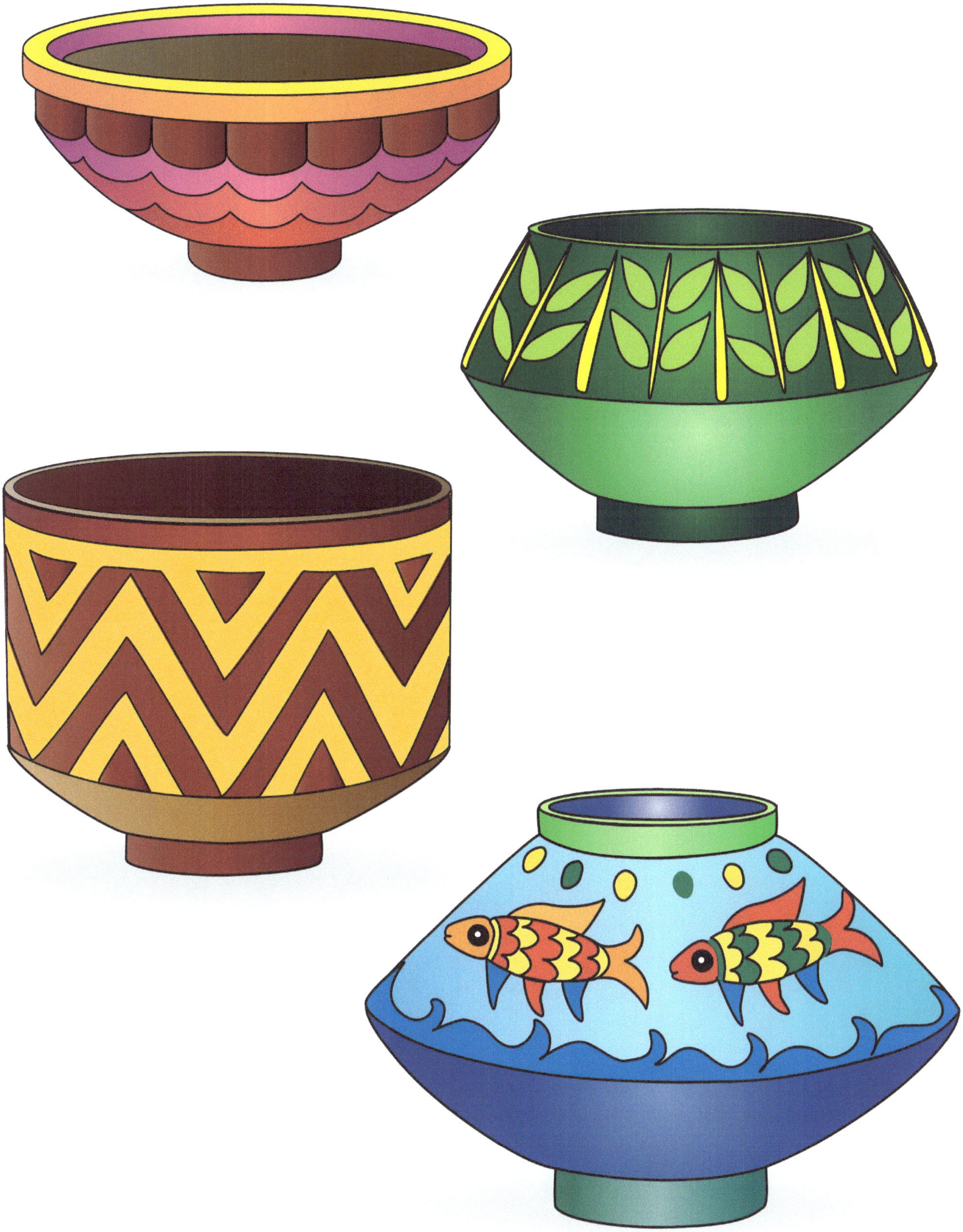

Potteries found in the Harappan Civilization were textured and painted. 4th Millennium B.C.E.

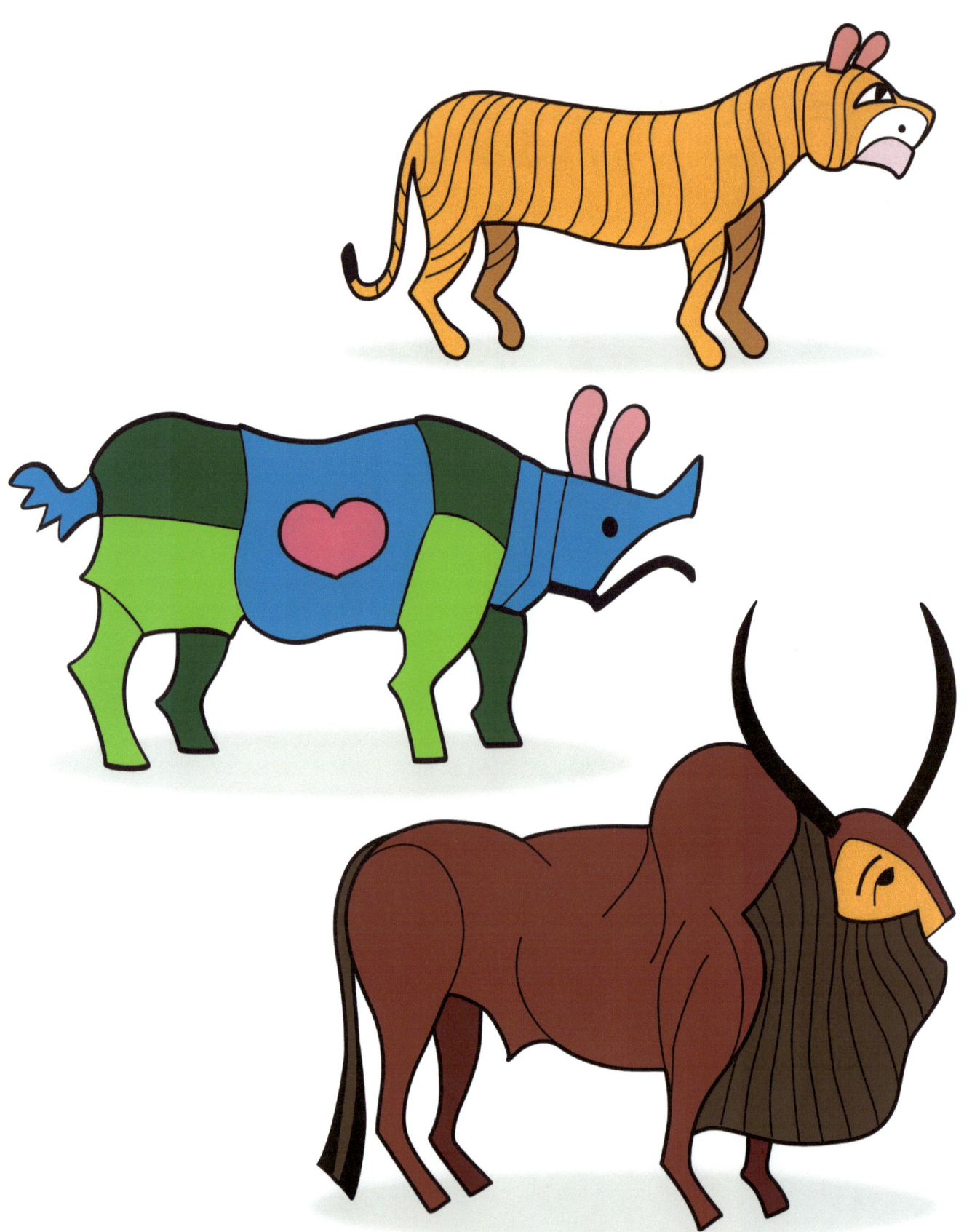

Animal characters as a bull, a tiger, and Indian rhinoceros are engraved in tiny seals found in the Harappan Civilization. Over 5000 years old.

Indian Art

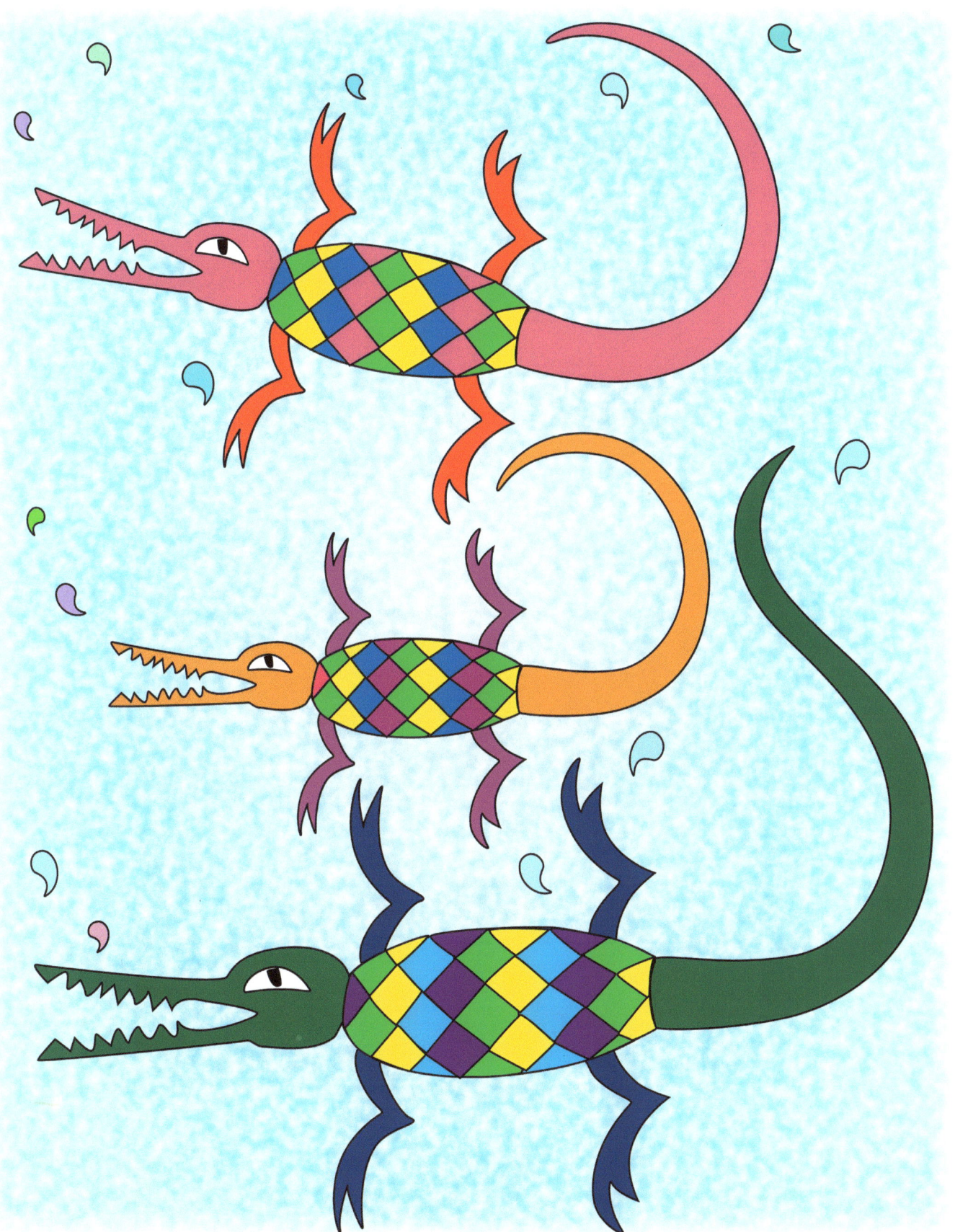

Stylized animal 'Gharial' engraved in seal found at Mohenjo-Daro in the Harappan Civilization. Over 5000 years ago.

Mithila art. Bihar, India.

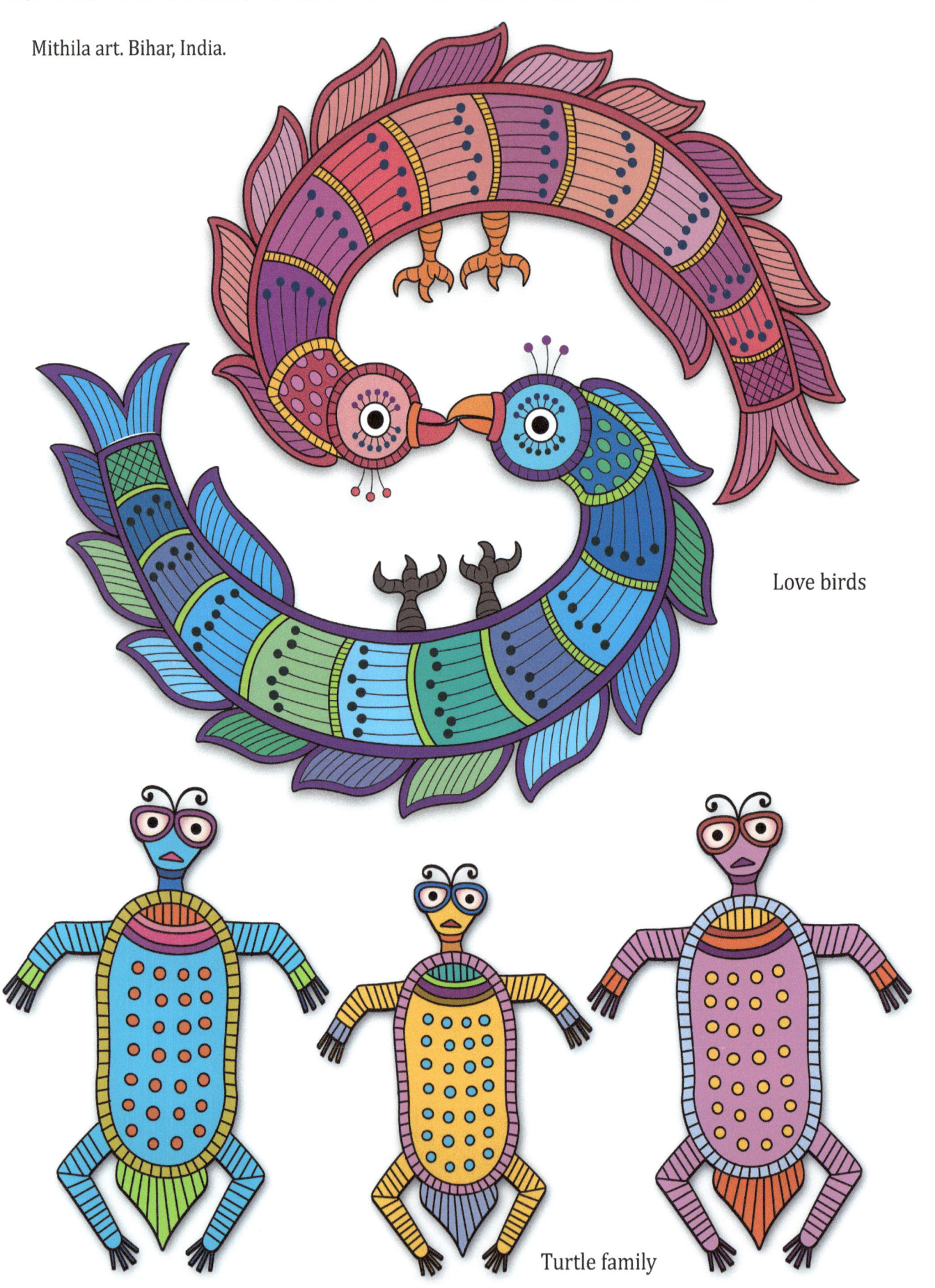

Love birds

Turtle family

Indian Art

Mithila art. Bihar, India.

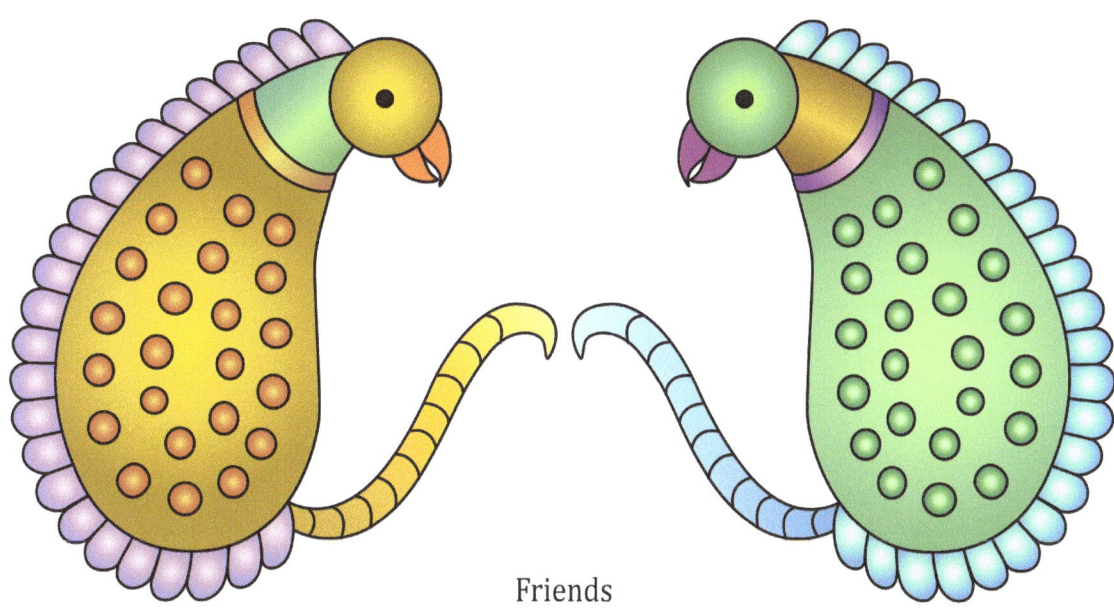

Friends

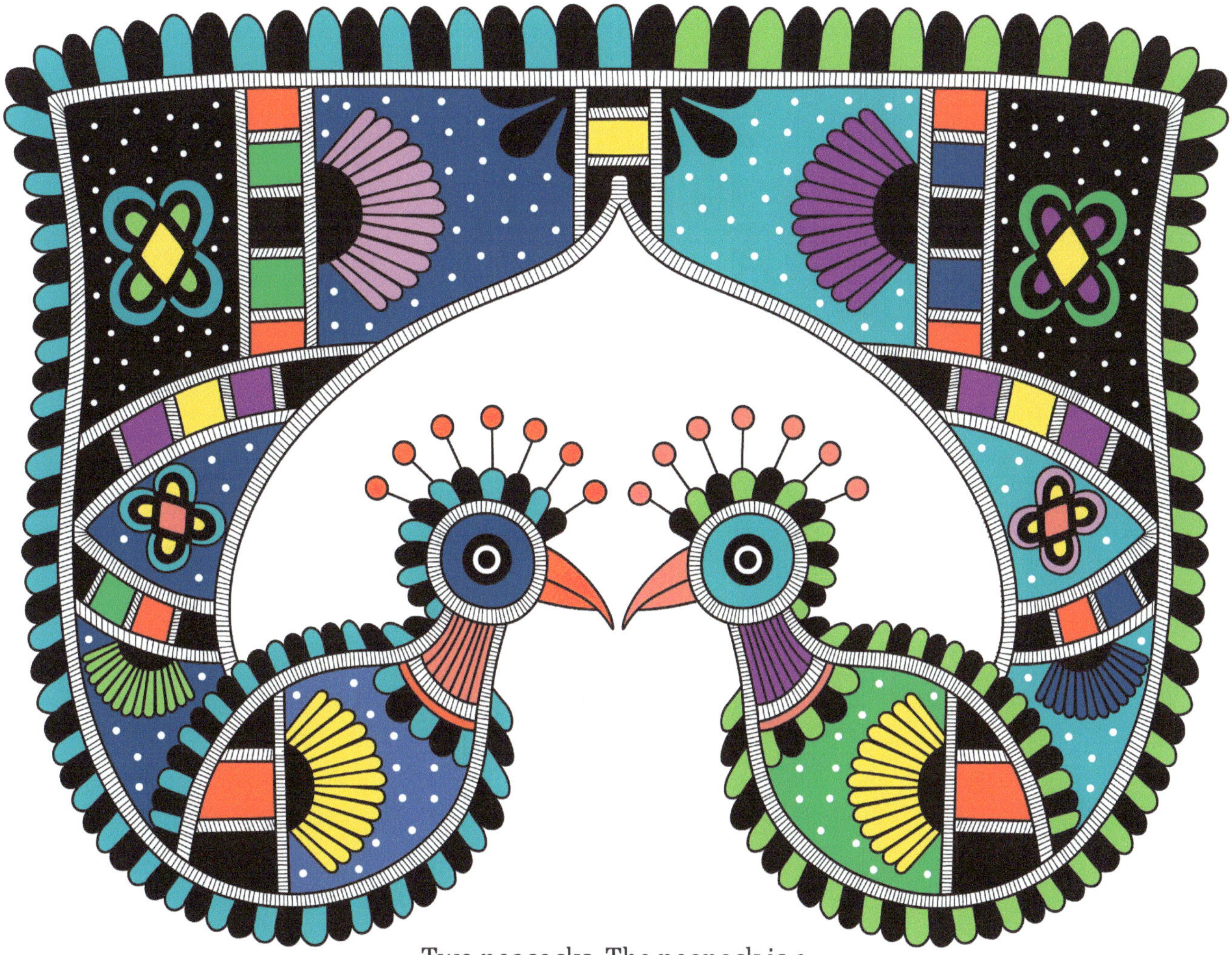

Two peacocks. The peapock is a
symbol of eternity in Mithila paintings.

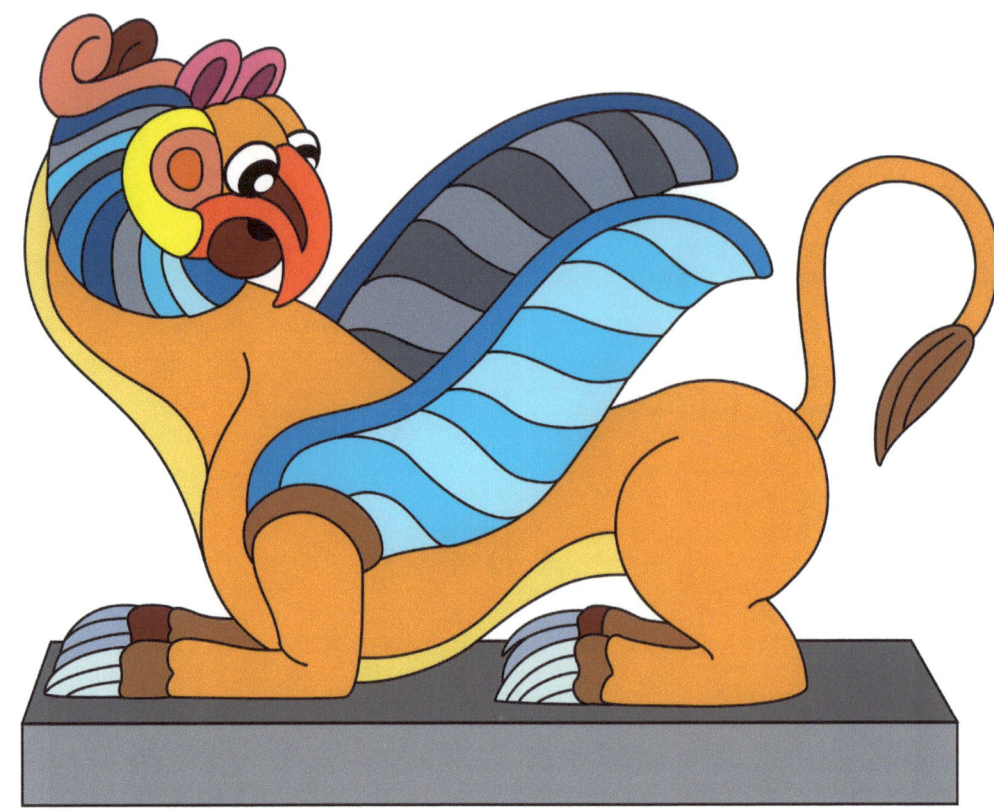

Griffin on the upper portion of a railing post on the Stupa of Saints, Sanchi. The second half of 2nd Century B.C.E.

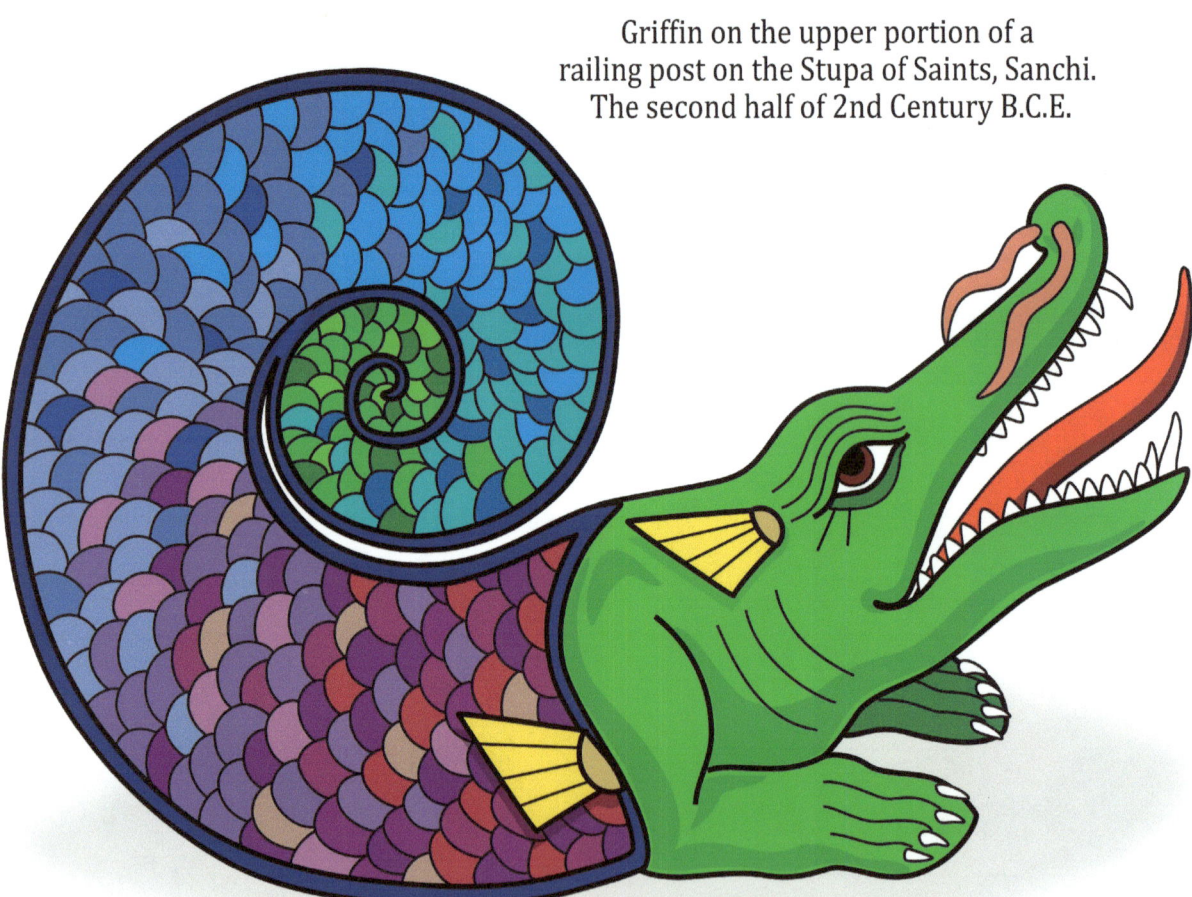

Makara, on the beam of gateway of Stupa of Bharhut. About 100 B.C.E.

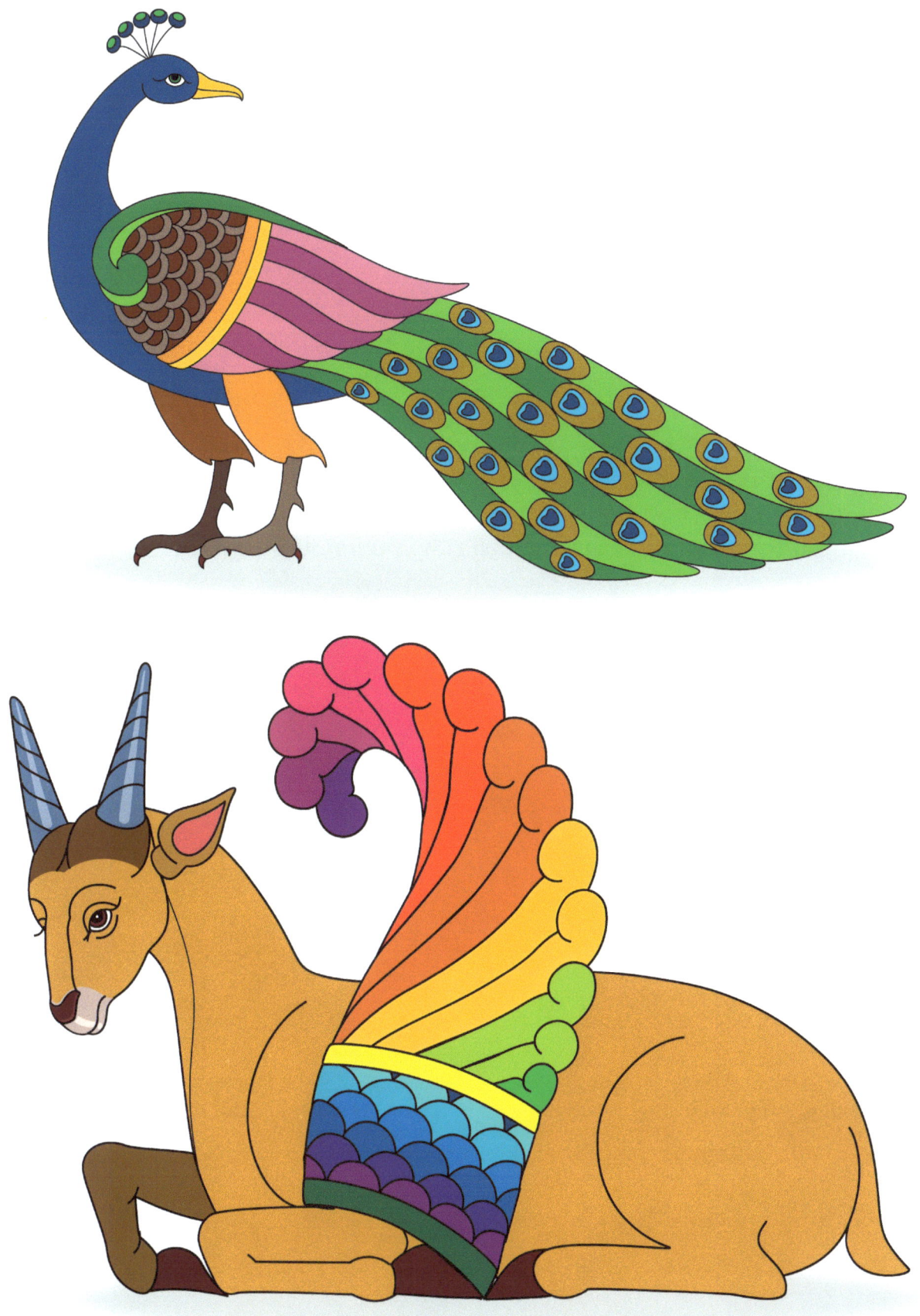

Peacock, and a mythical creature from the great Stupa of Sanchi, 1st Century B.C.E.

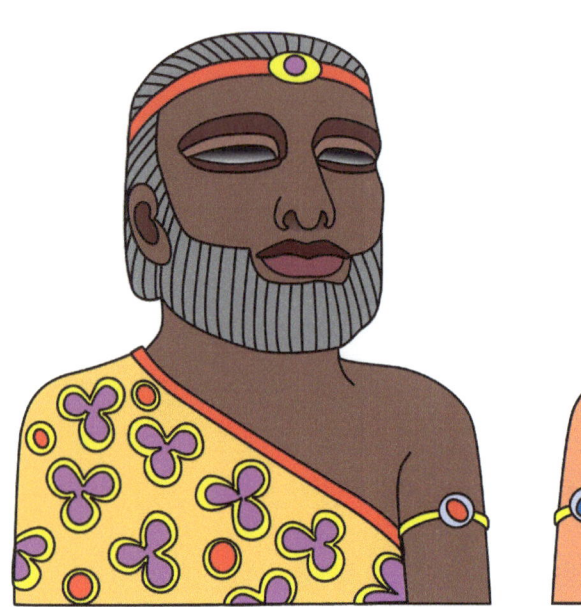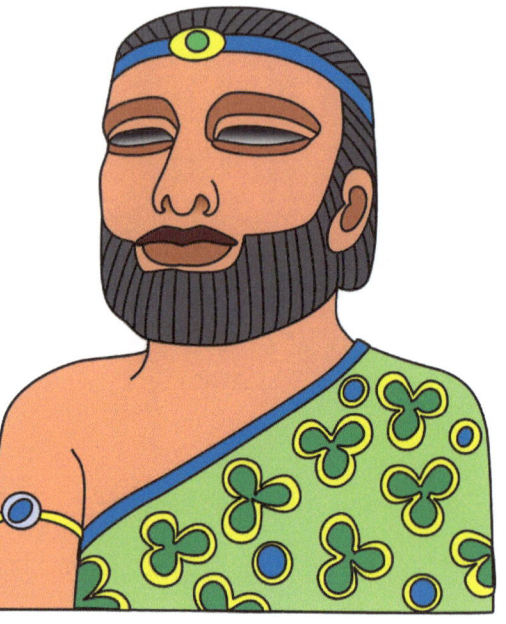

Head of a bearded man was found carved on limestone during excavation of the Harappan Civilization, 3000 B.C.E.

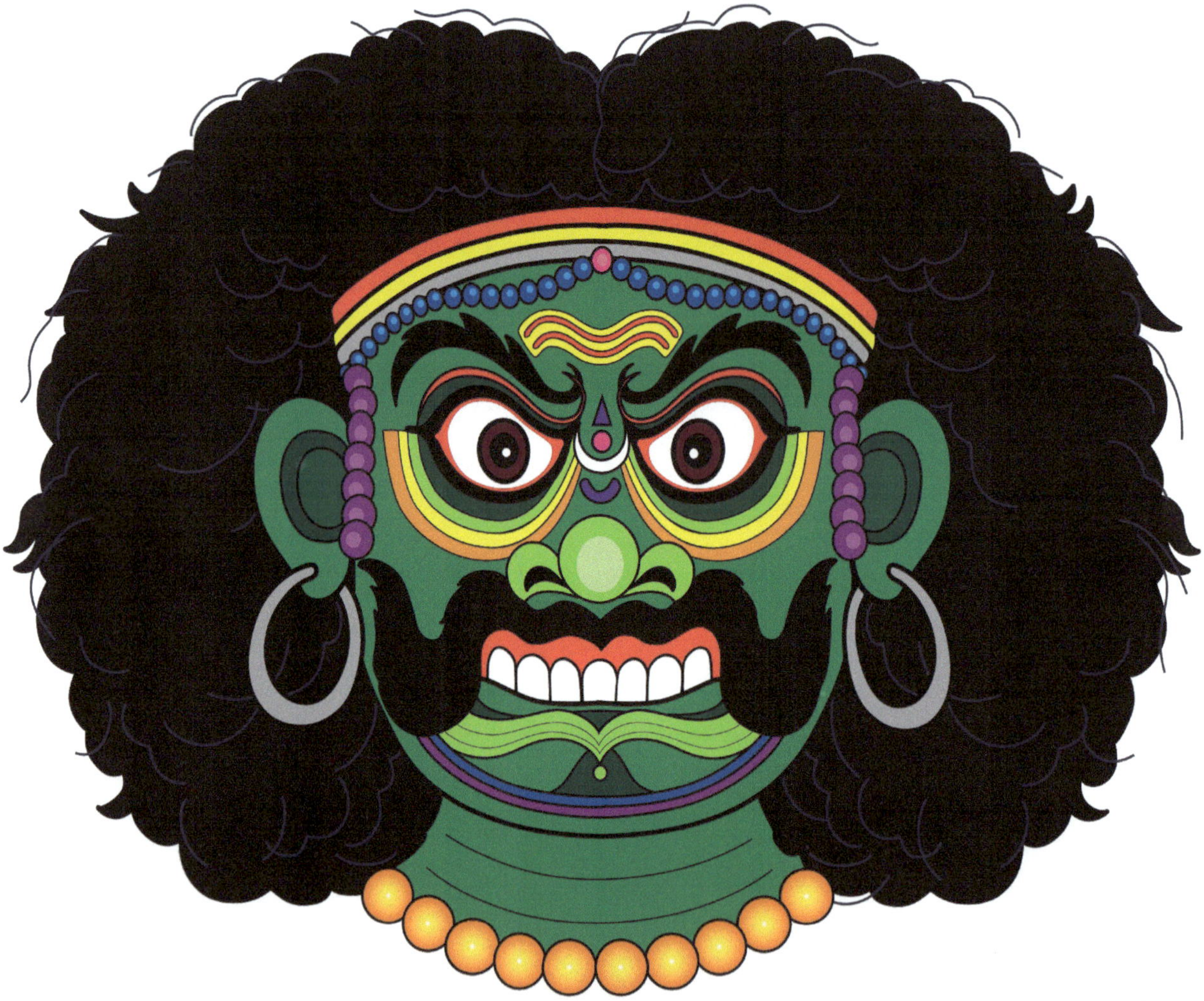

Mask of a Demon from traditional folk dance. Bengal, India.

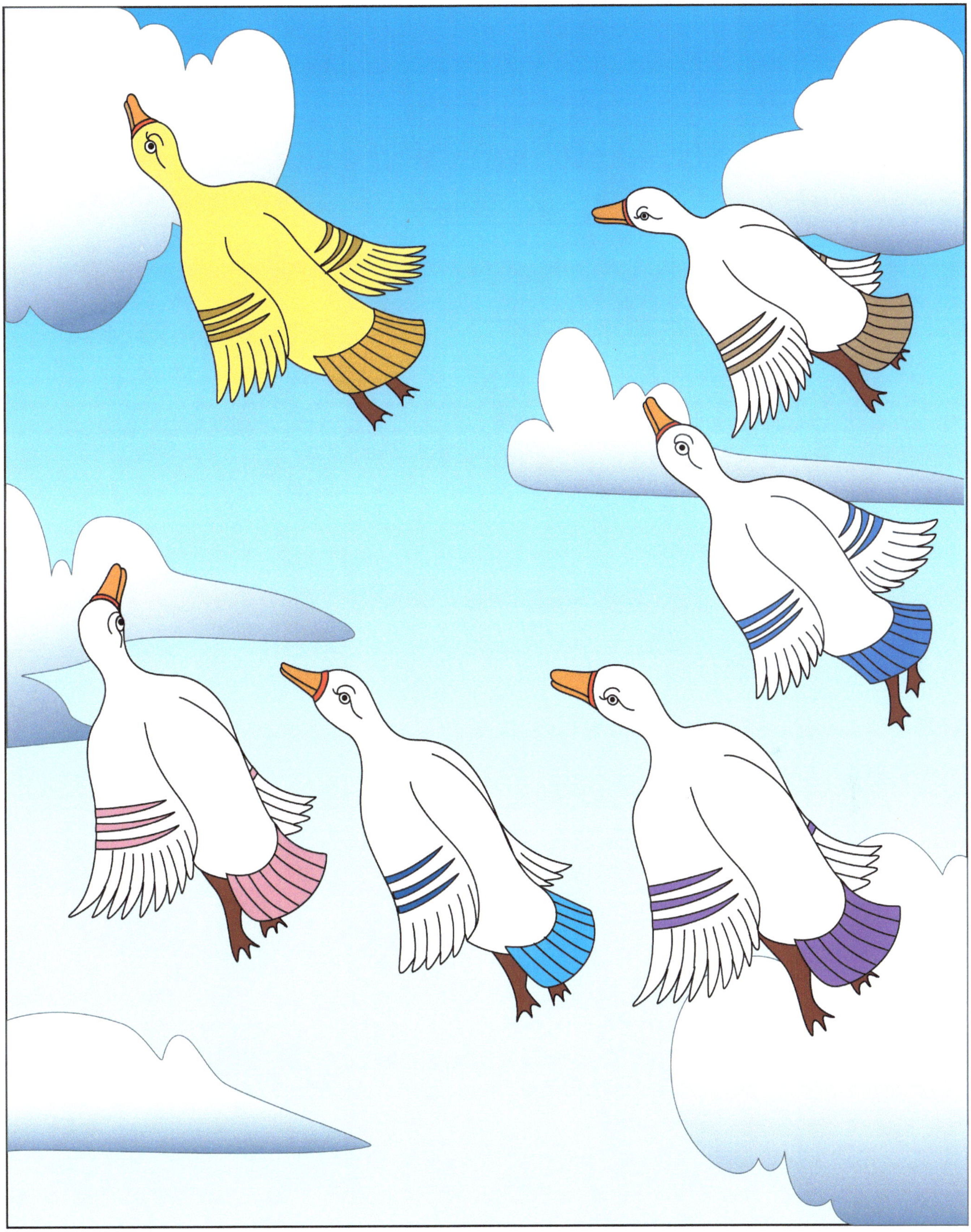

Golden Goose. The king of the Geese from Hamsa Jataka.
Ajanta Cave Painting. Middle of 5th Century C.E.

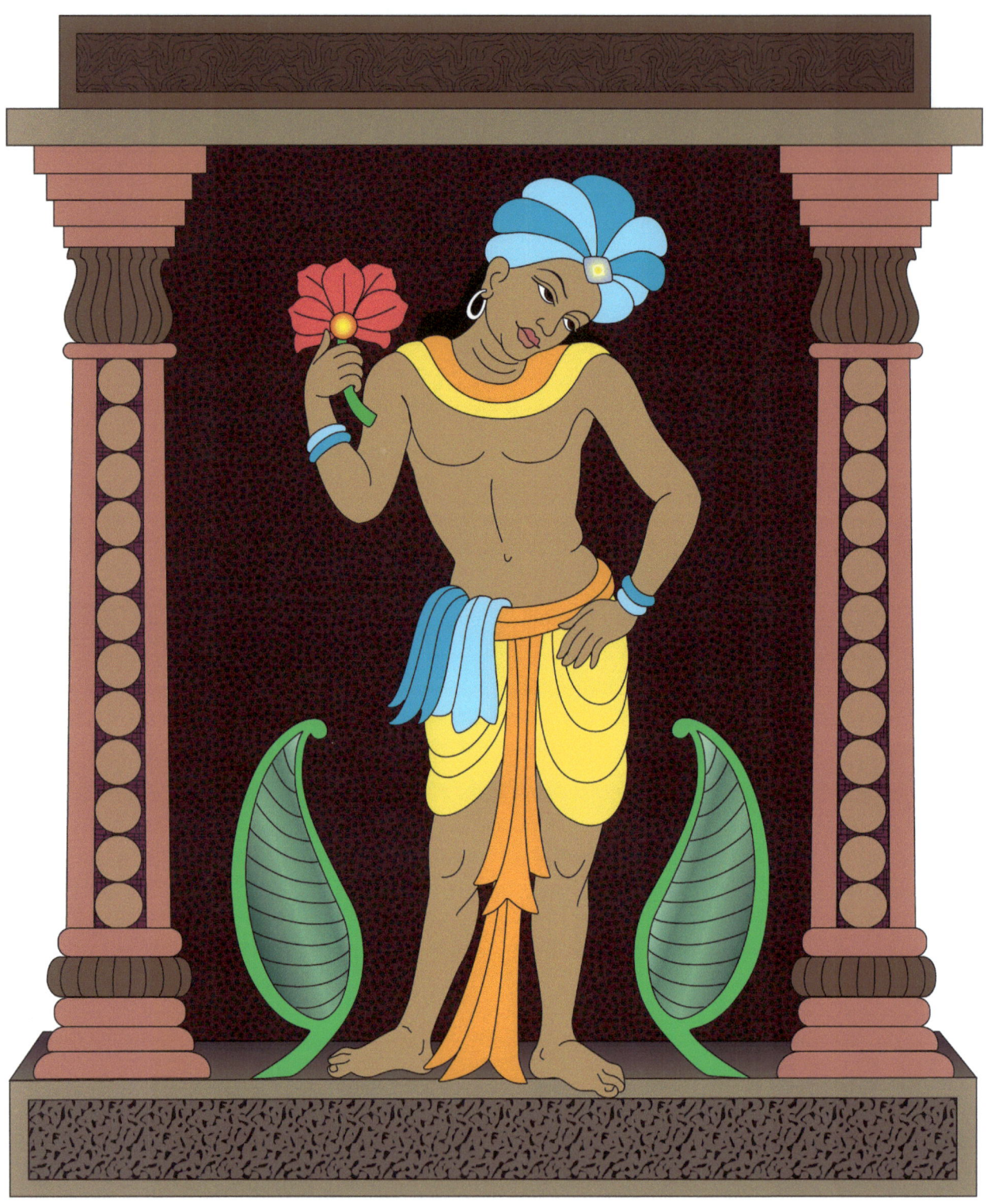

Relief work on marble from Stupa of Amravati. Andhra period, 2nd Century C.E.

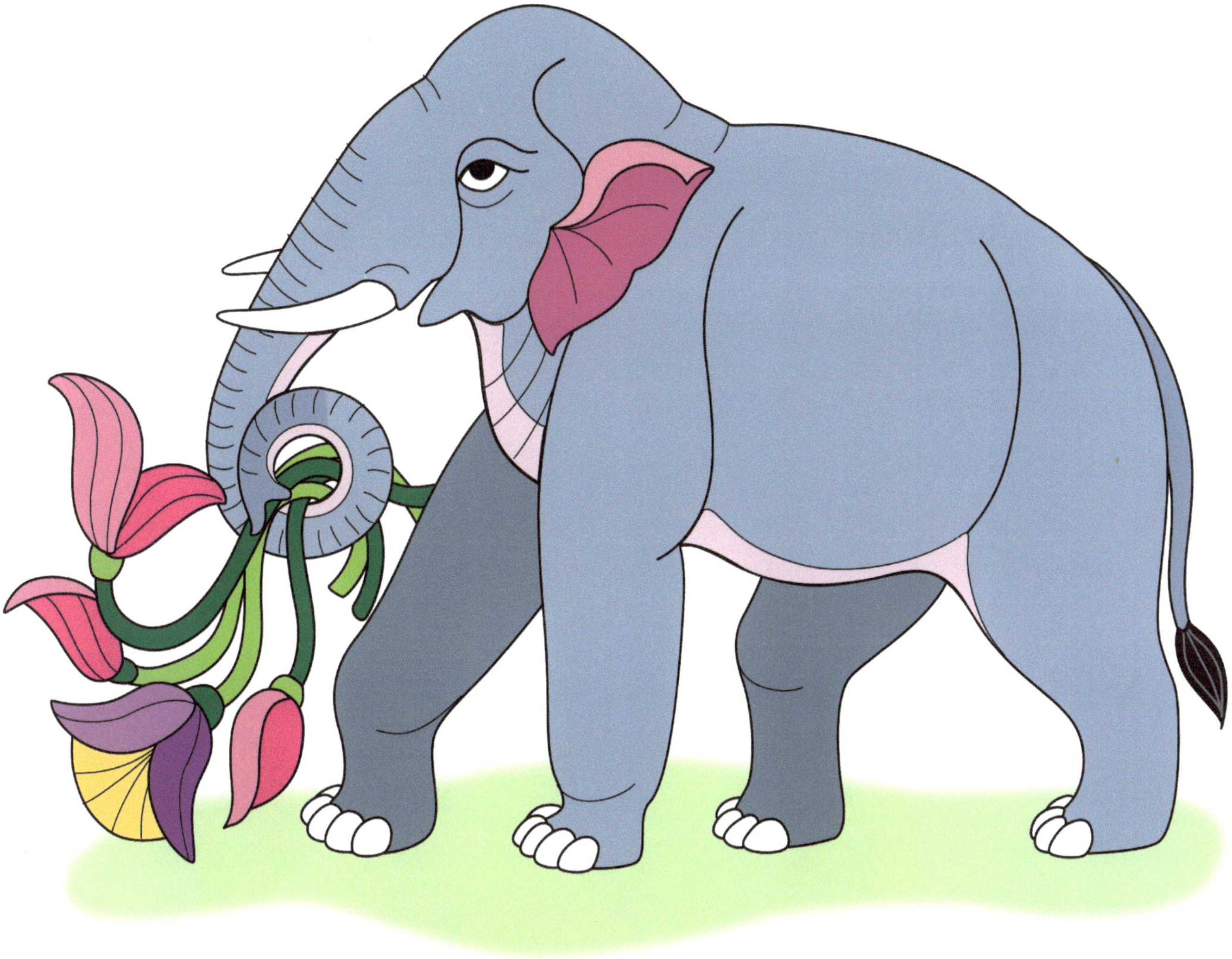

On the carvings of Sanchi Pillar, Sandstone, 1st Century, B.C.E. Flowers, birds and beasts, reflecting the closeness which the Indians have always felt for the world of nature.

In Indian art we find an intimate relation between the world of physical beauty and the world of spirit.

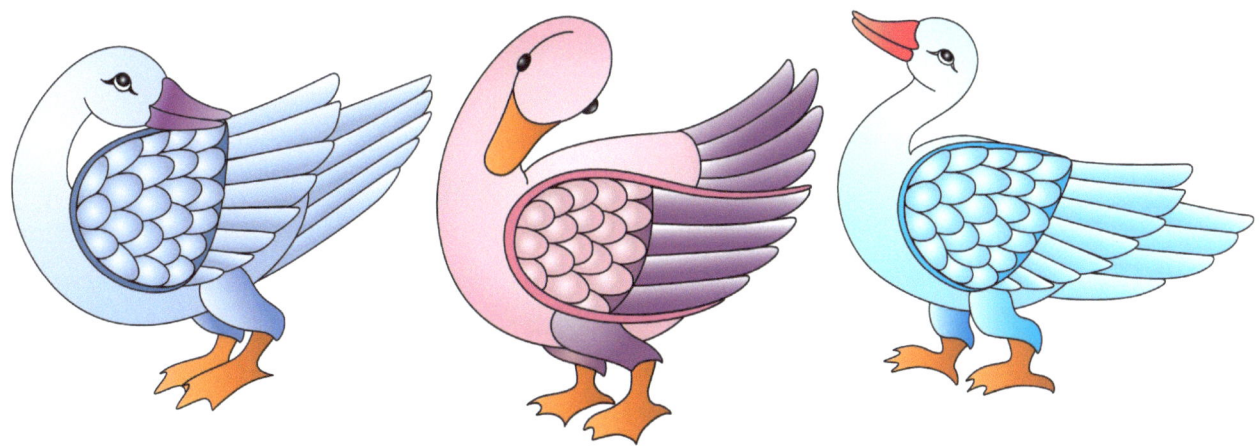

Ducks on one of the Sanchi Pillers (toranas). 1st Century C.E.

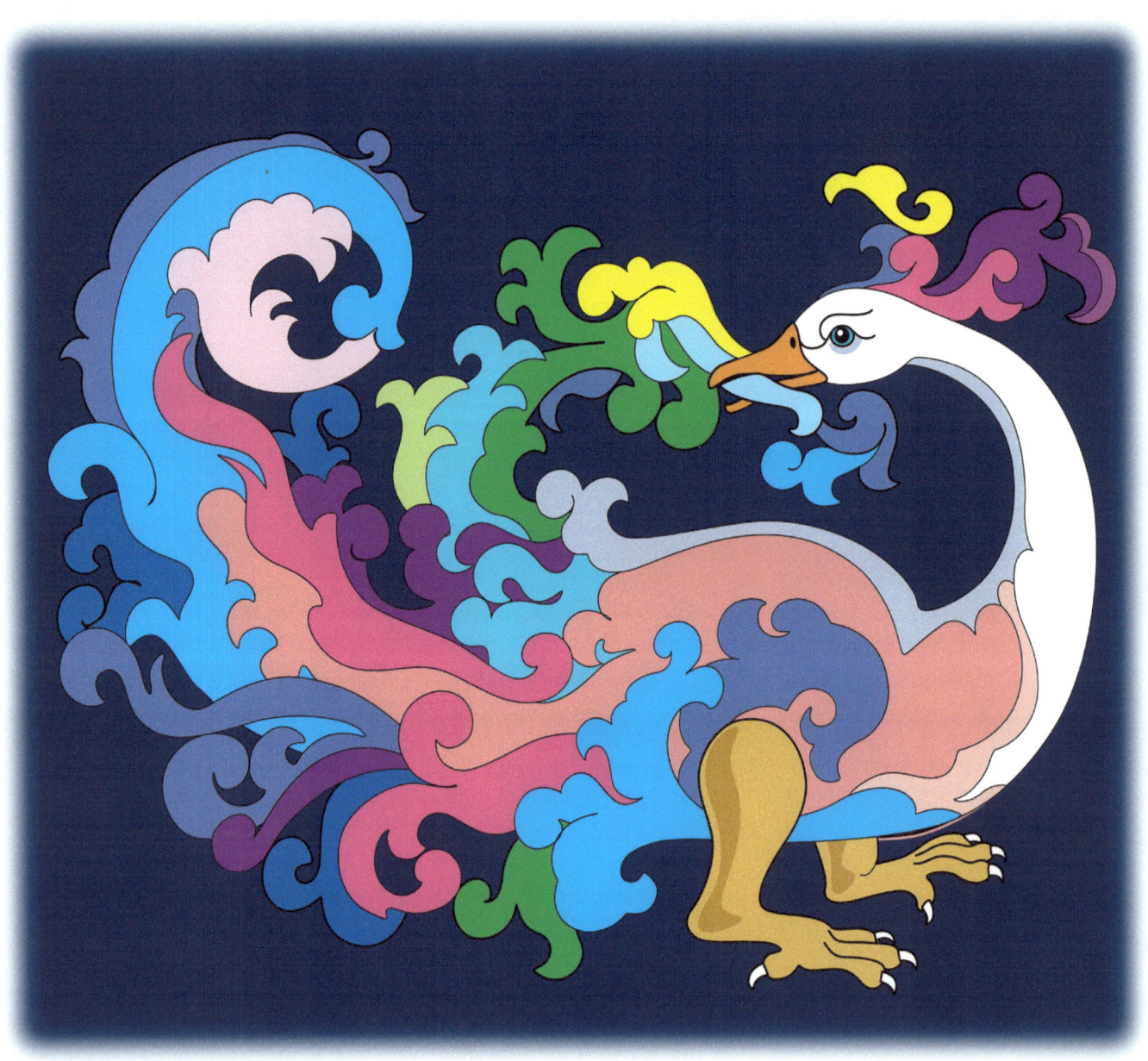

Hamsa, beautiful and stylized relief on
North wall of Virupaksha Temple, Pattadakal. Circa 740 C.E.

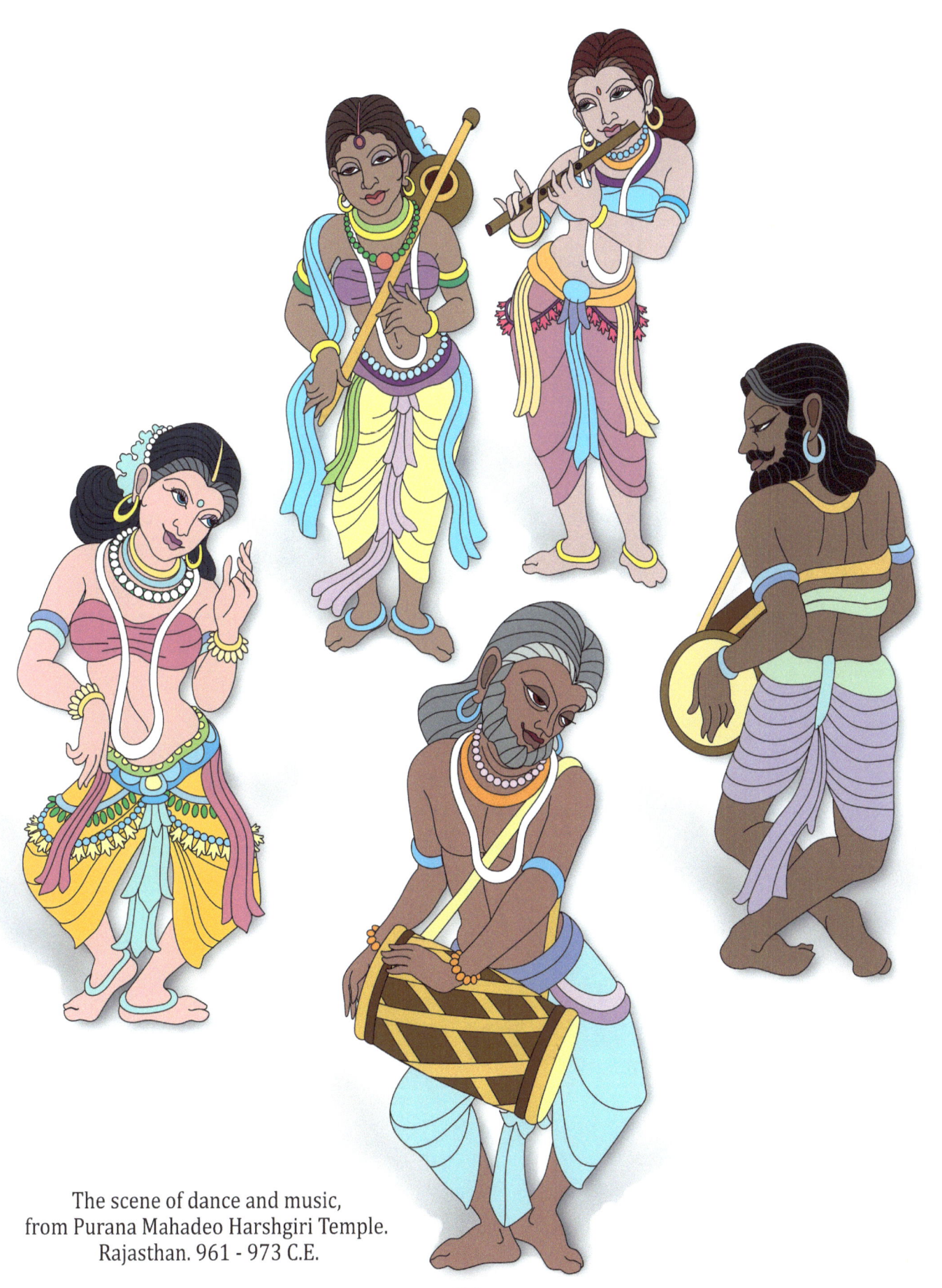

The scene of dance and music, from Purana Mahadeo Harshgiri Temple. Rajasthan. 961 - 973 C.E.

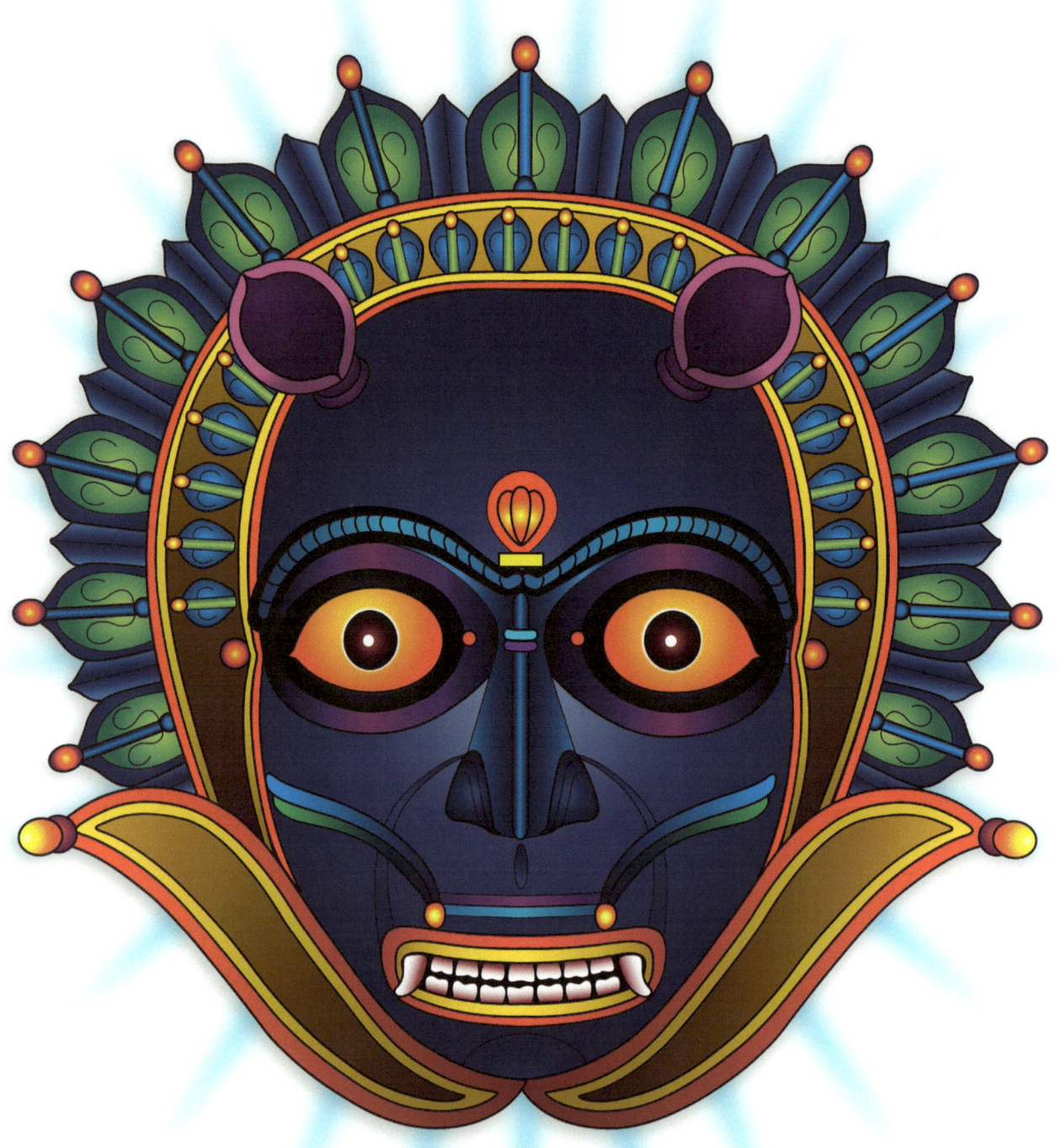

Demon (Bhuta) Mask with feline ears and whiskers, 19th Century bronze from South India. The mask is worn by dancers during religious festivals. It is believed, the demon comes to inhibit the body of the dancer and later slain by the mother goddess herself.

Indian Art

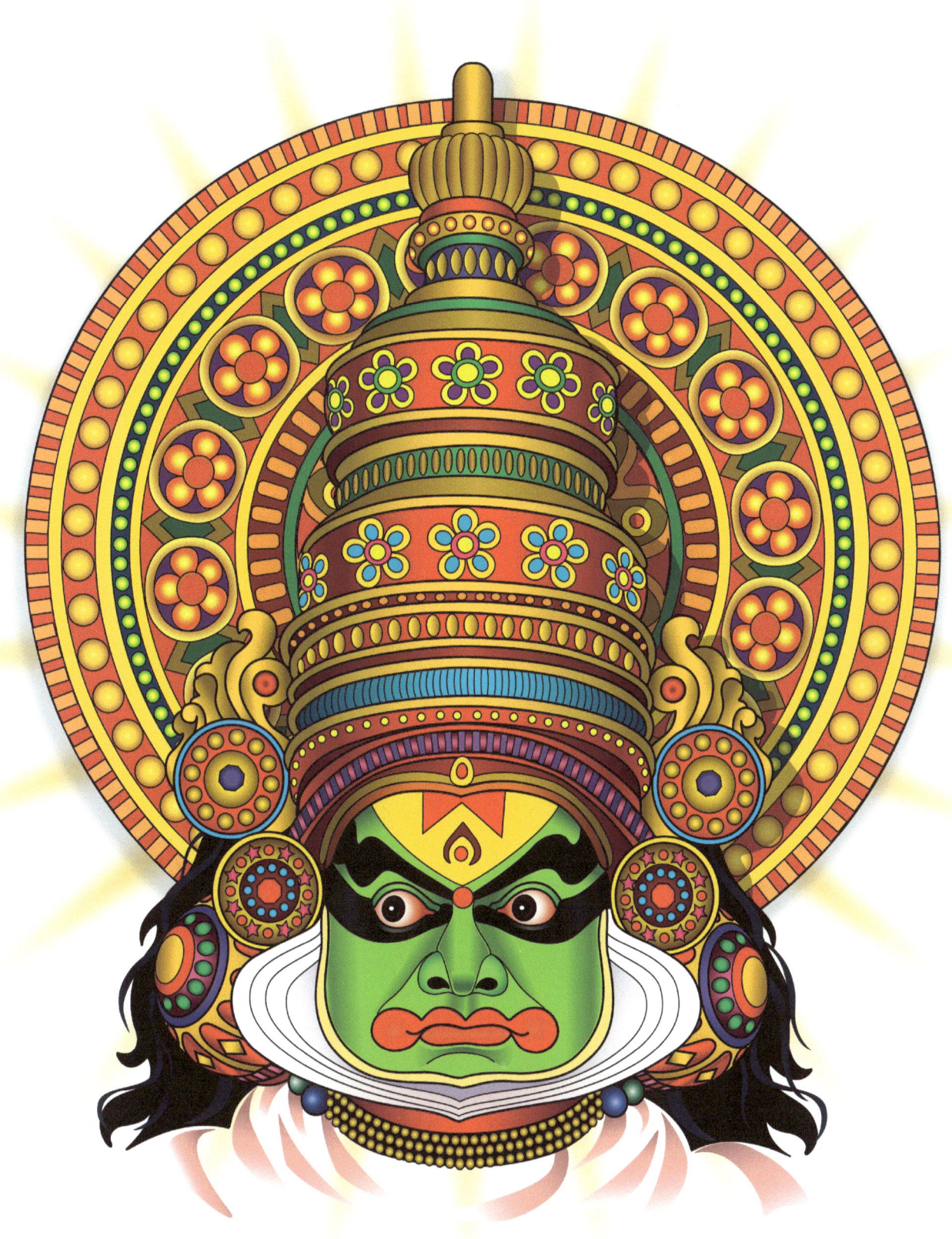

Kathakali performer with make up and costumes. Kathakali- literally means 'Story-Play,' well known classical dance-drama from South Indian state of Kerala. It dates back to 17th Century C.E.

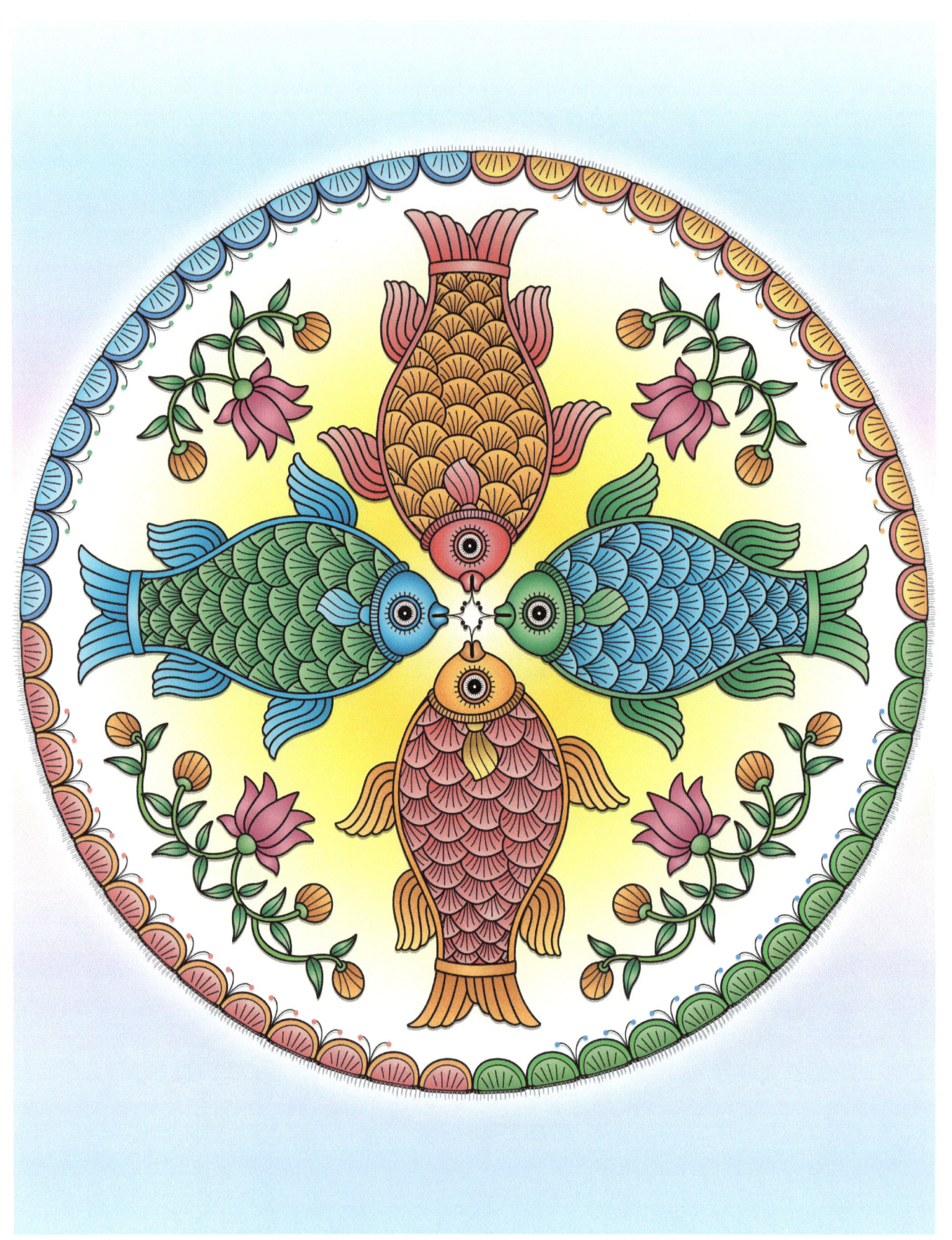

Mithila painting with fish aripana, depicting the cycle of life.

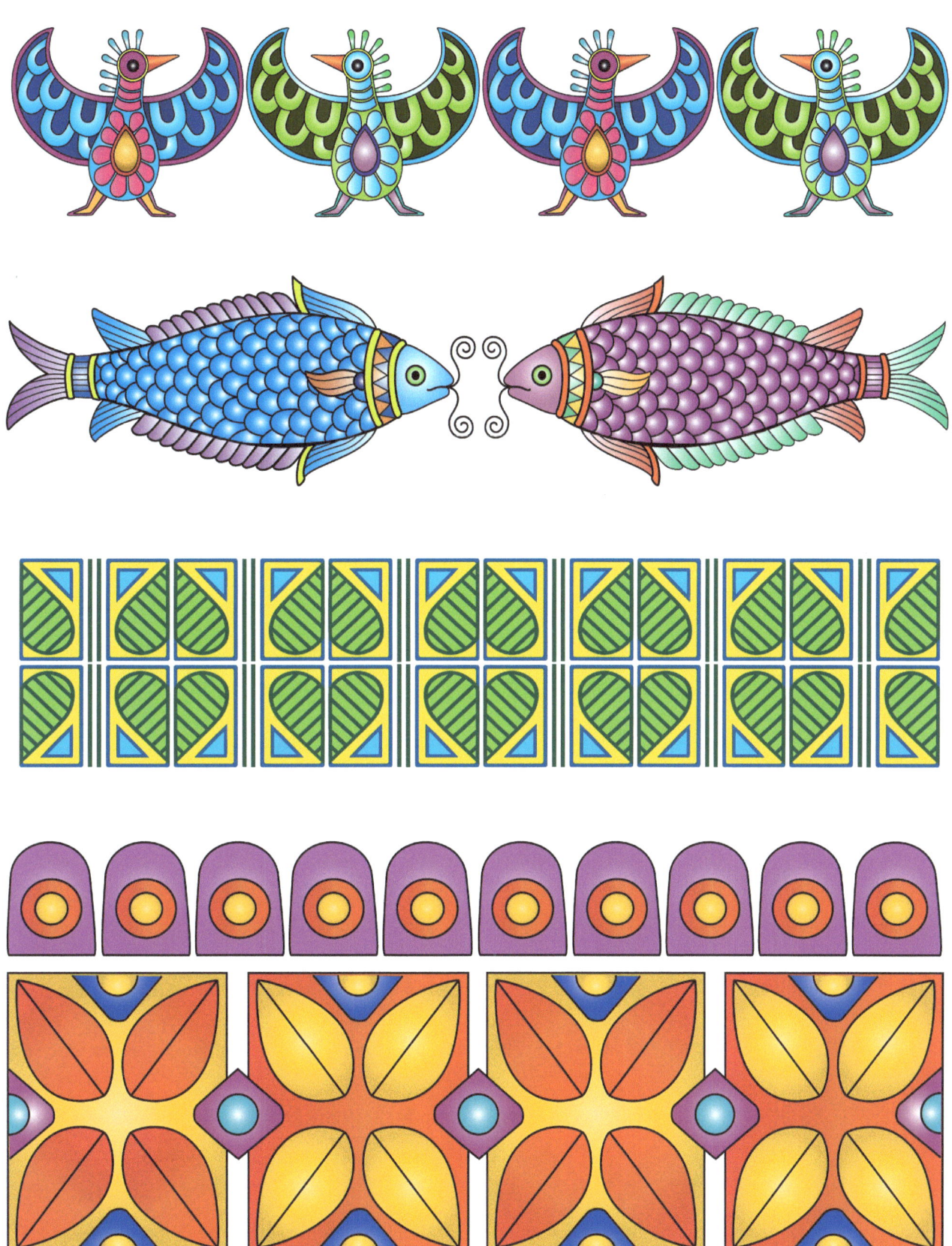

Examples of images created using the elements found in Indian Art.

A LOOK INTO
Cambodian art

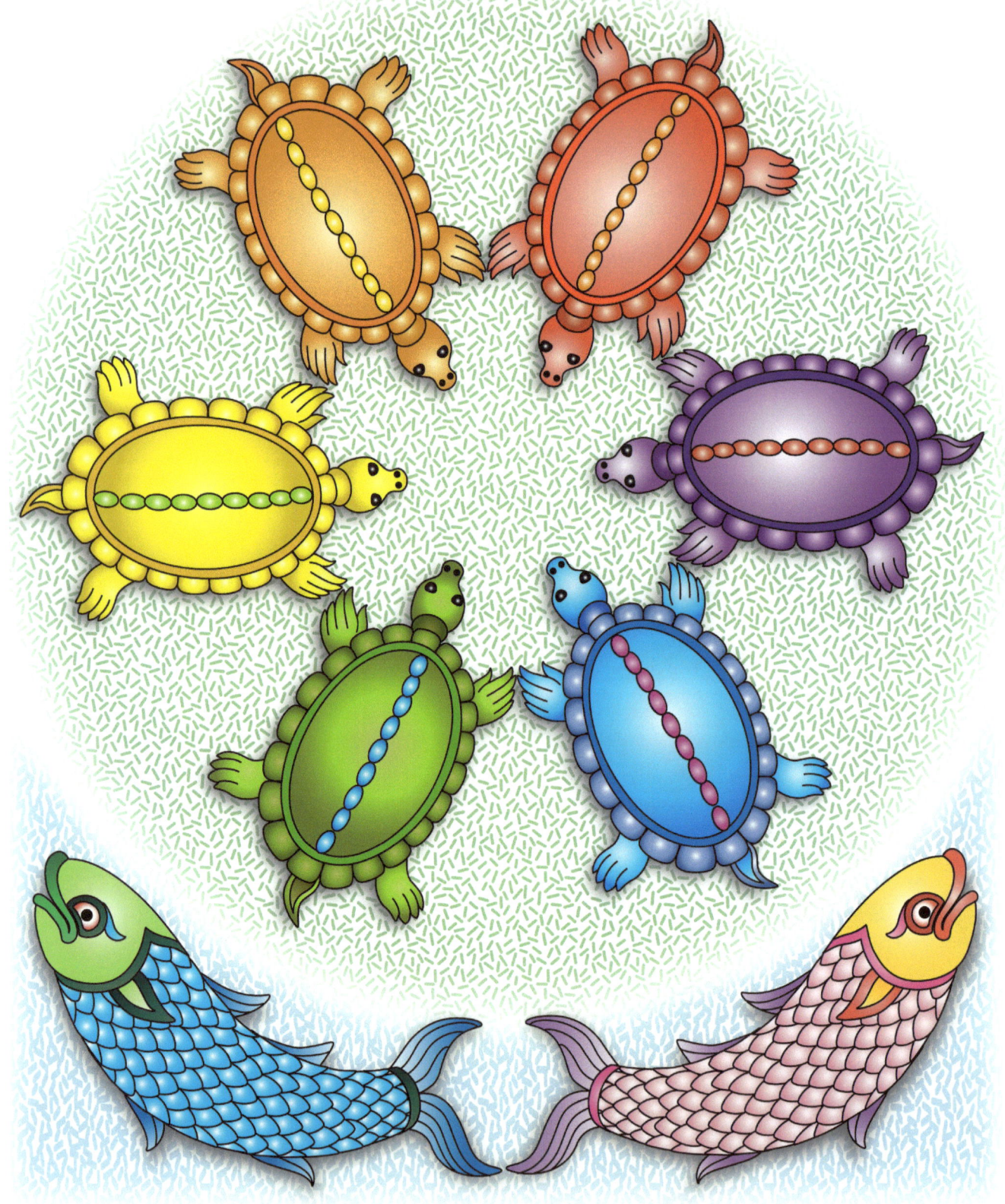

Fish and turtle on bas-relief. Angkor Wat.

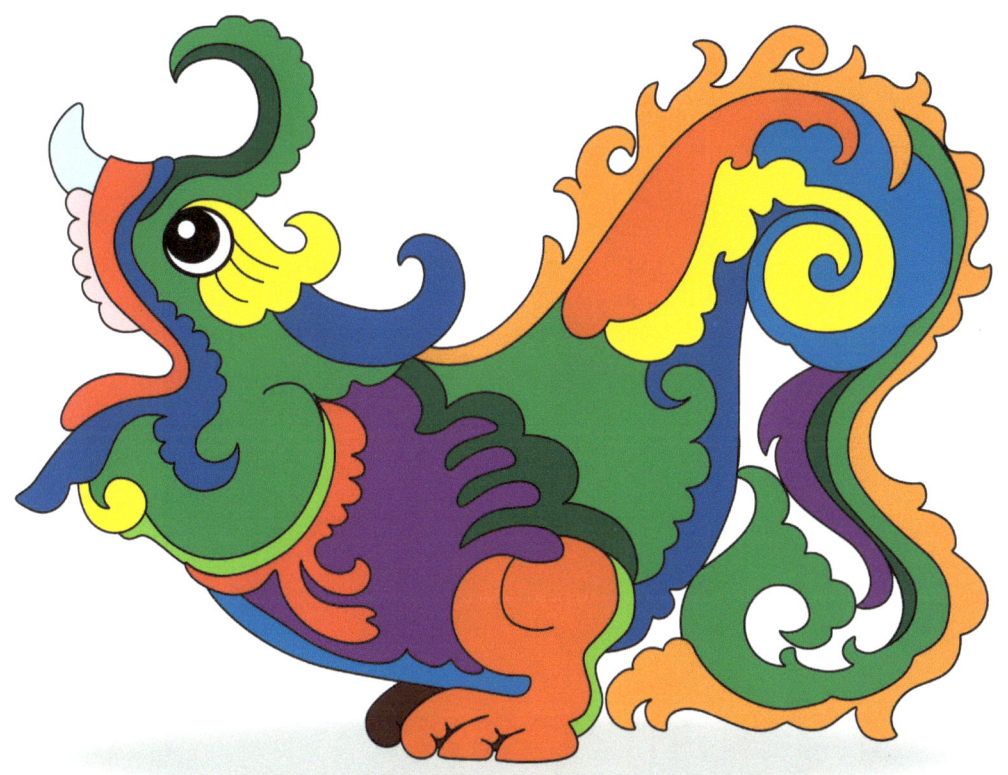

Probably Makara, a fabulous animal. Banteay Srei, Angkor Thom.

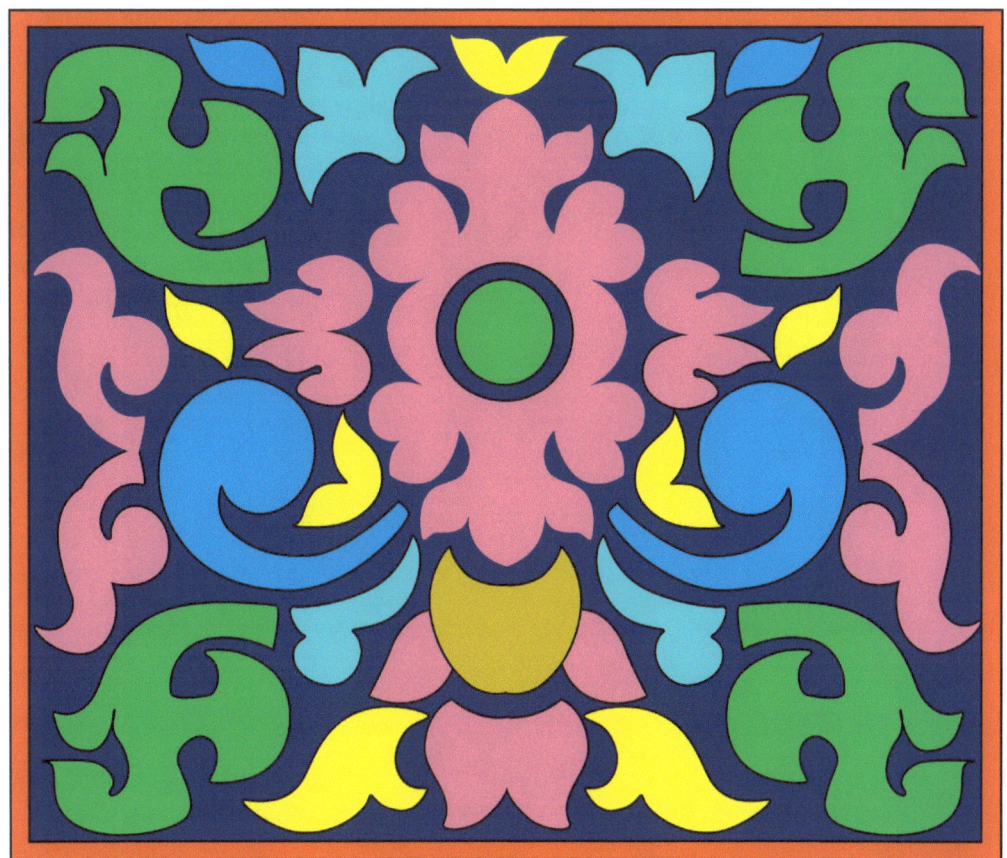

Floral designs in decorative carvings in the temple complex of Prasat Thom, north of Angkor. Circa 921 C.E.

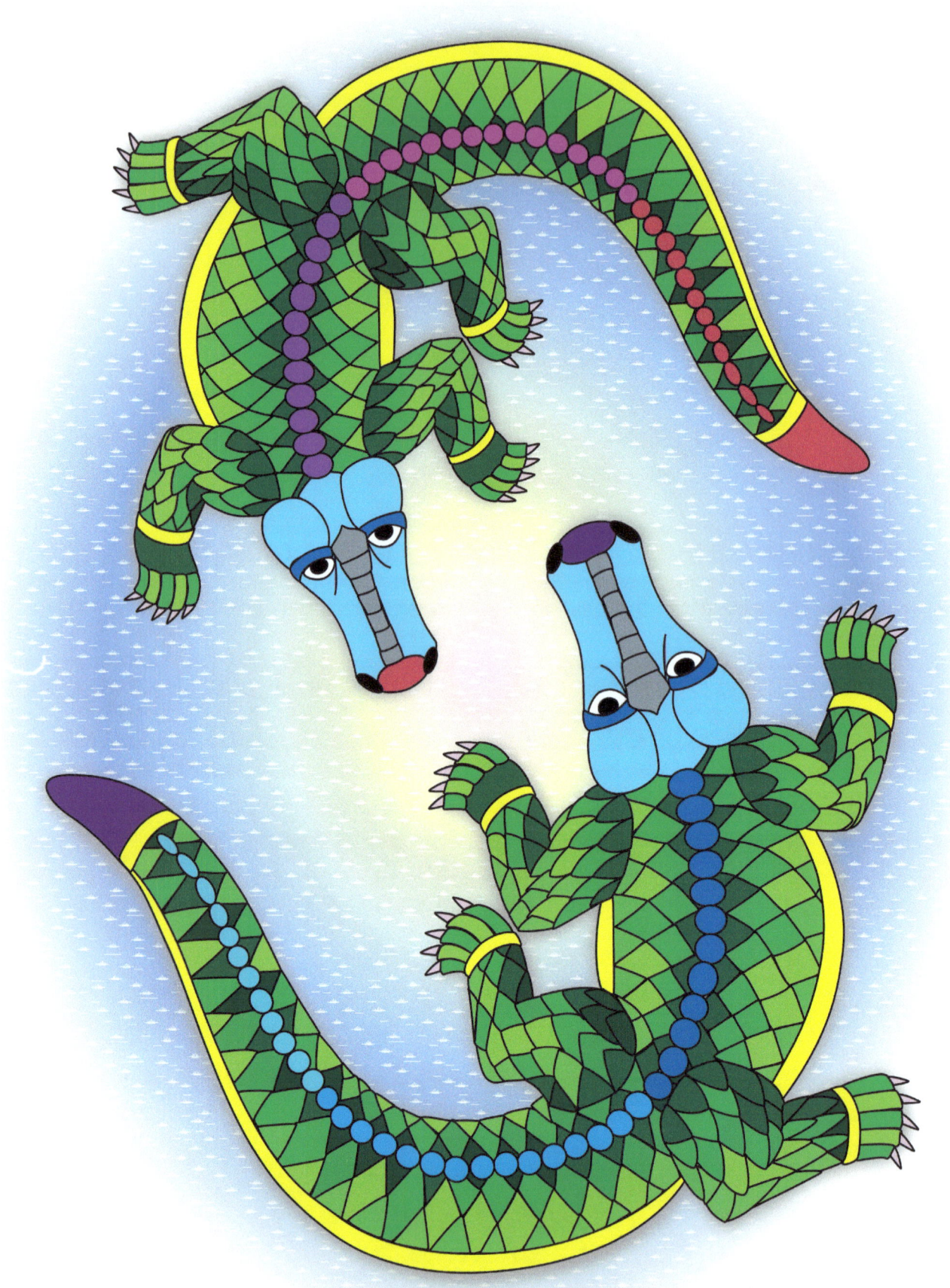

Crocodiles on a bas-relief in the outer gallery of the temple at Angkor Thom (first half of 13th Century C.E.).

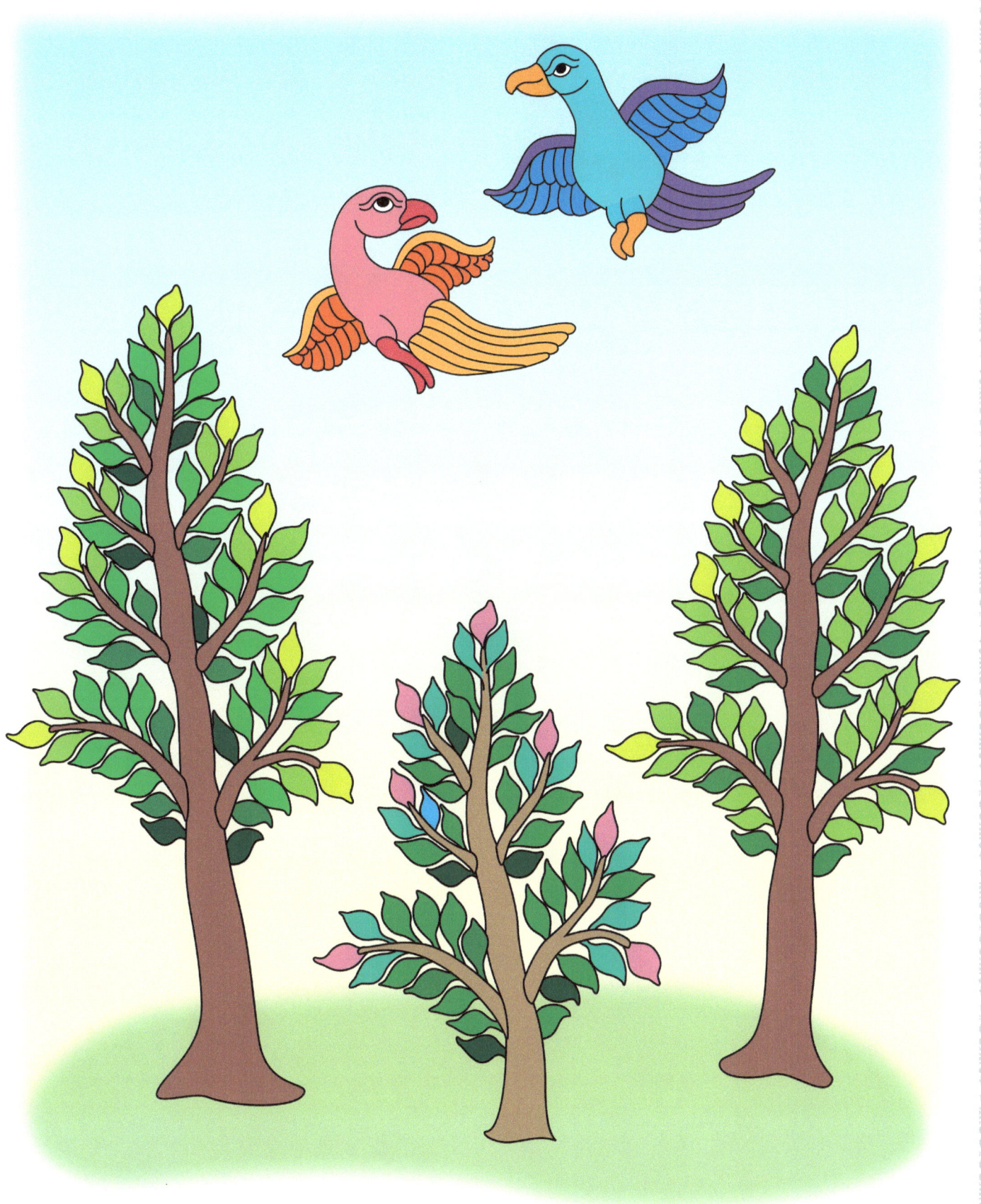

Birds and trees from reliefs of the eastern front
of the North 'library.' Banteay Srei, Angkor Thom. 967 C.E.

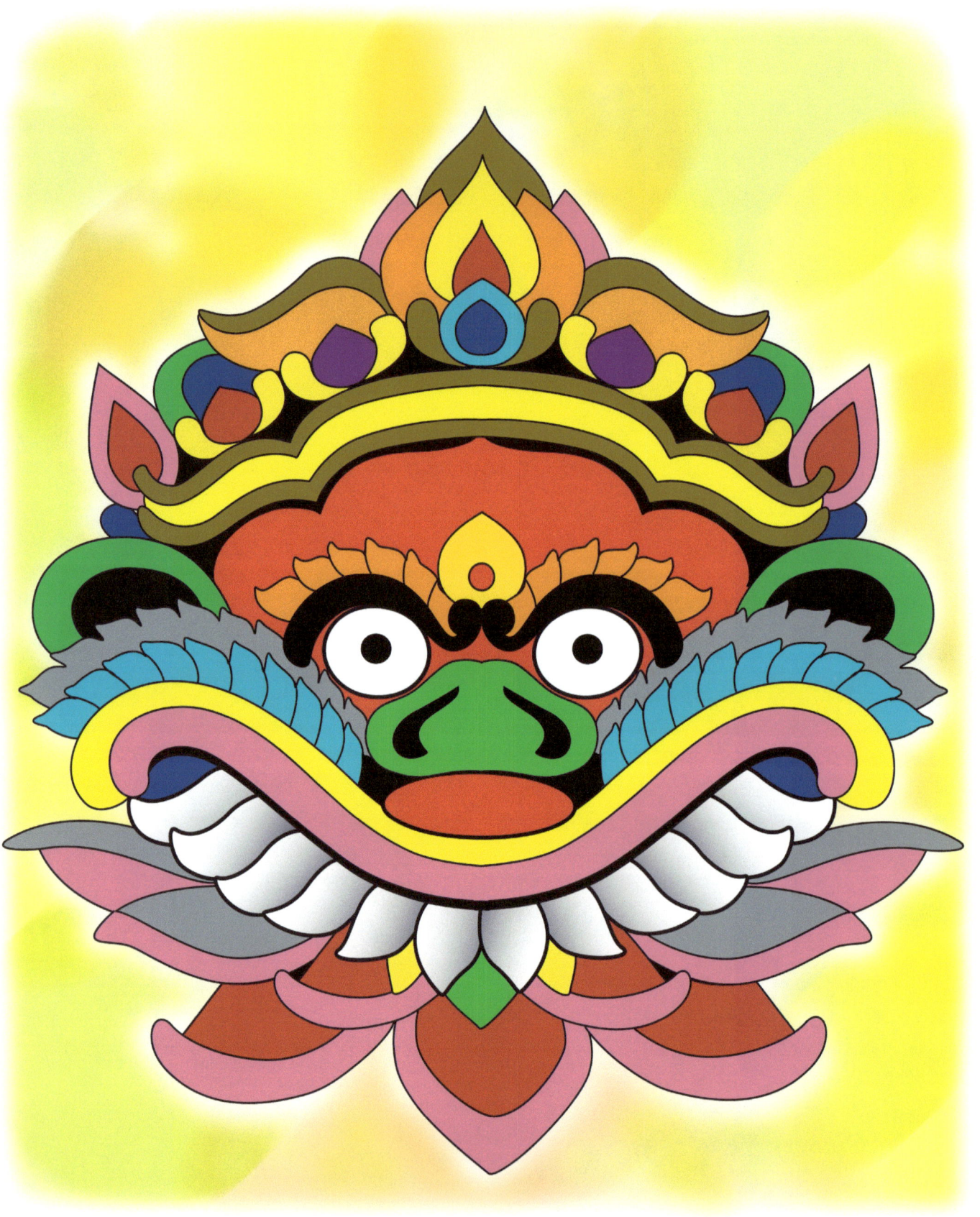

A Monster head from the gate
of a temple in Banteay Srei. Angkor Thom, 11th Century C.E.

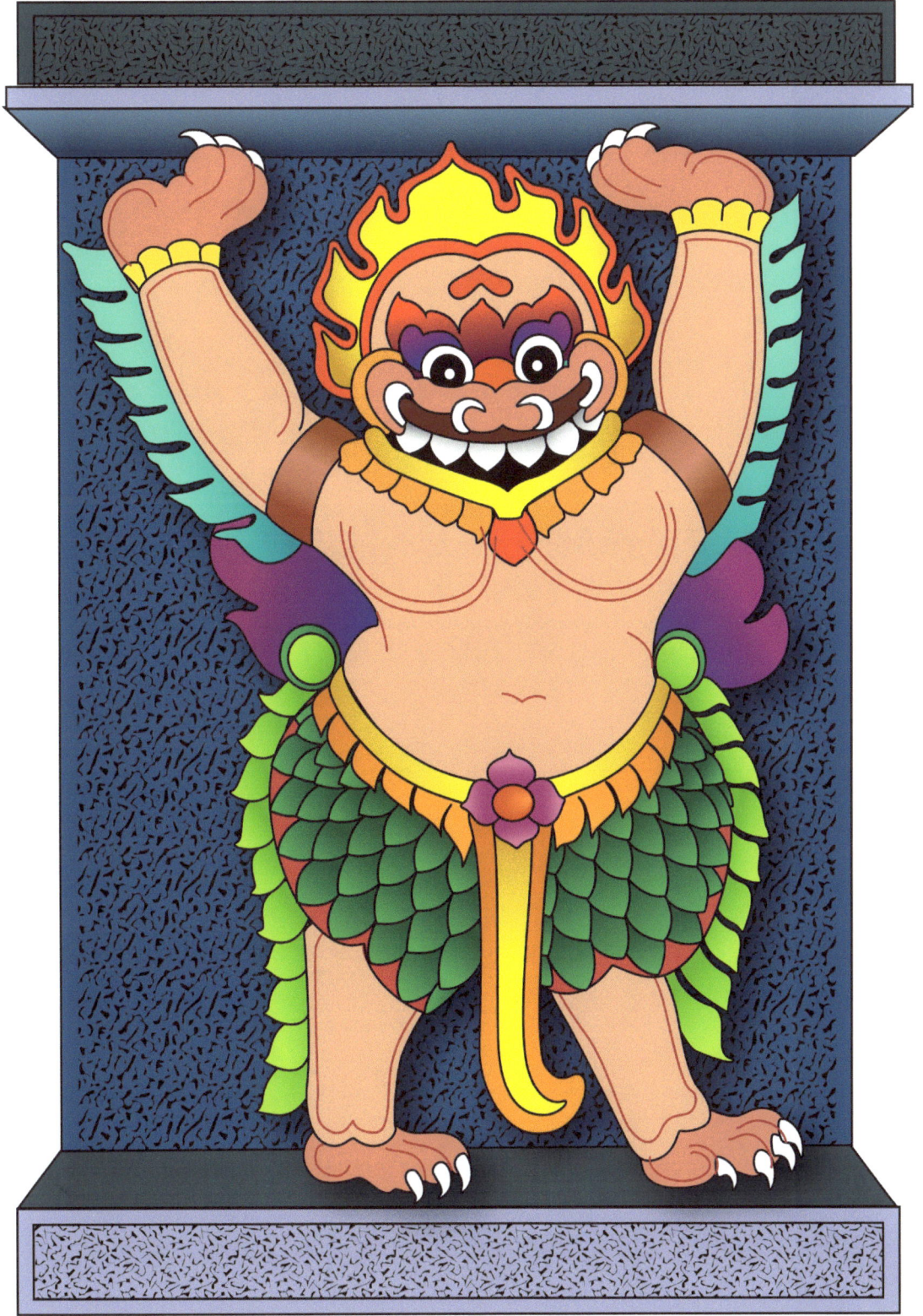

Figure of Garuda (a bird-headed deity) in the panel. Preah Khan, Angkor Wat.

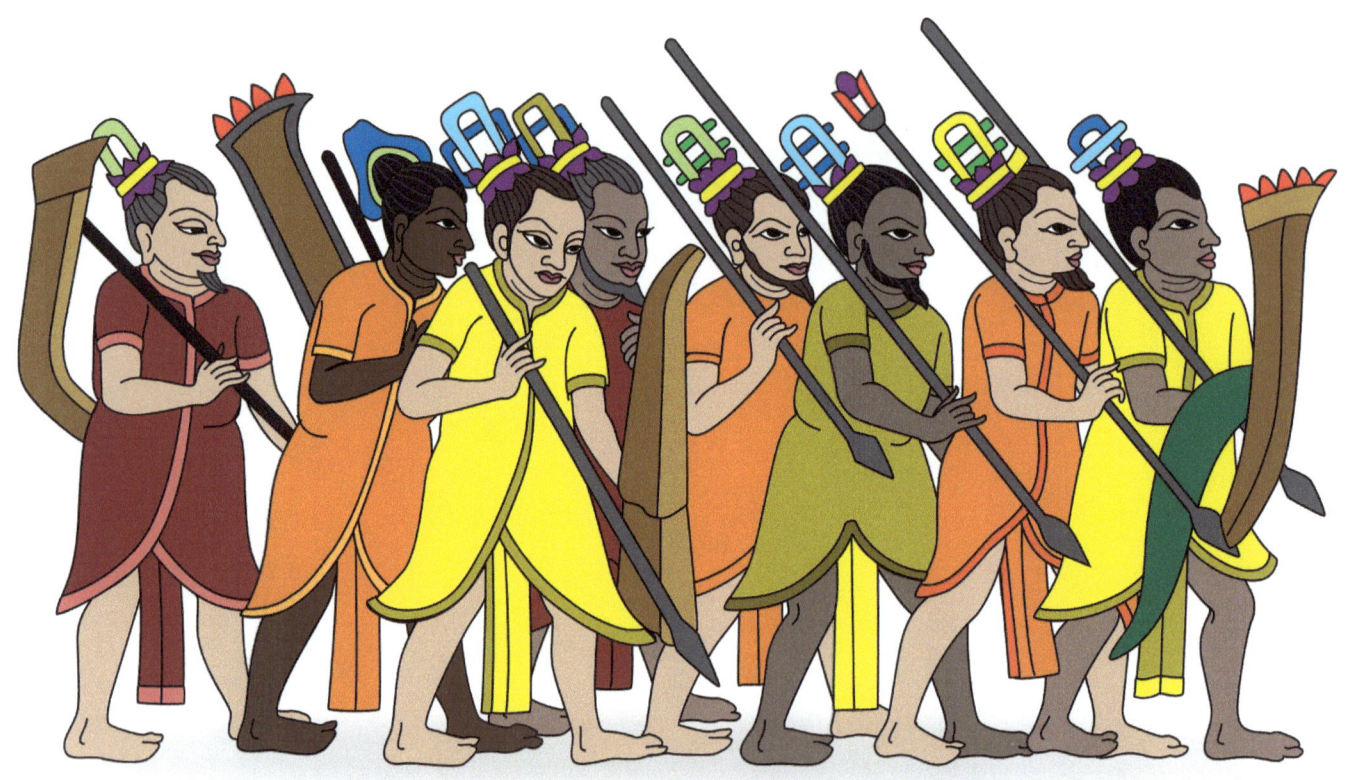

The army of Chams from the relief in the outer gallery.
The Bayon, Angkor Thom. Towards the end of 12th Century C.E.

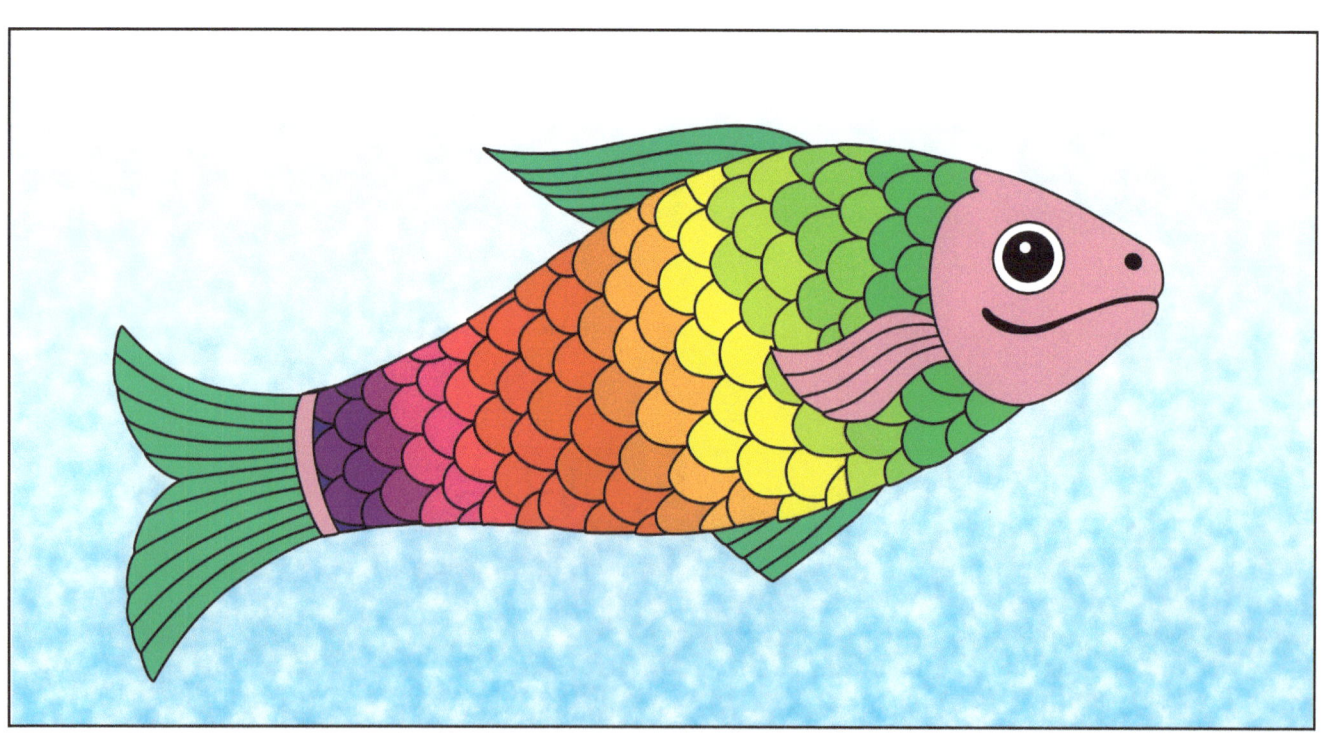

Swimming fish- from a bas-relief in scenes on day-to-day life at the Bayon, Angkor Thom.

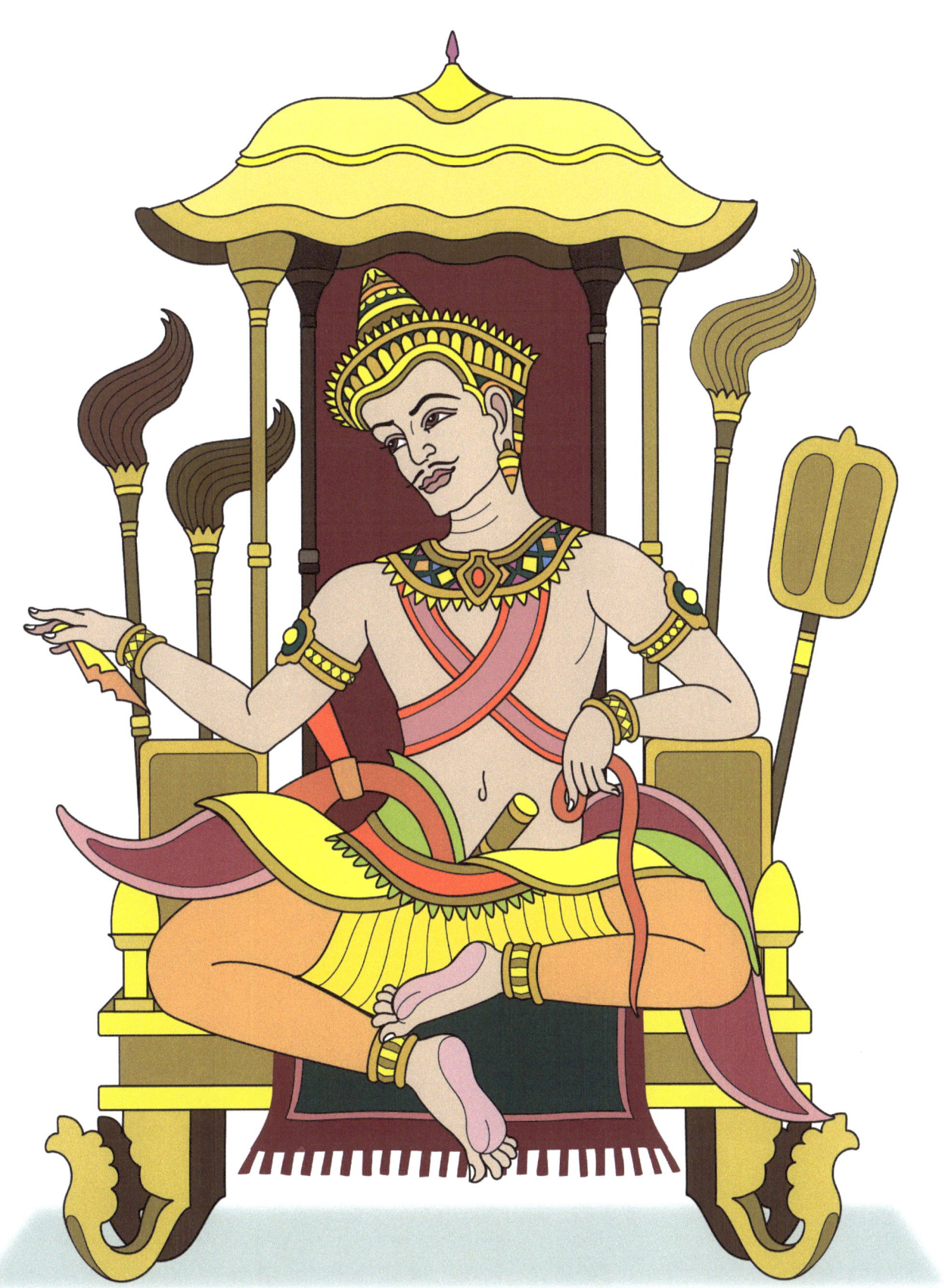

King Suryavarman -II in his throne. Angkor Vat.

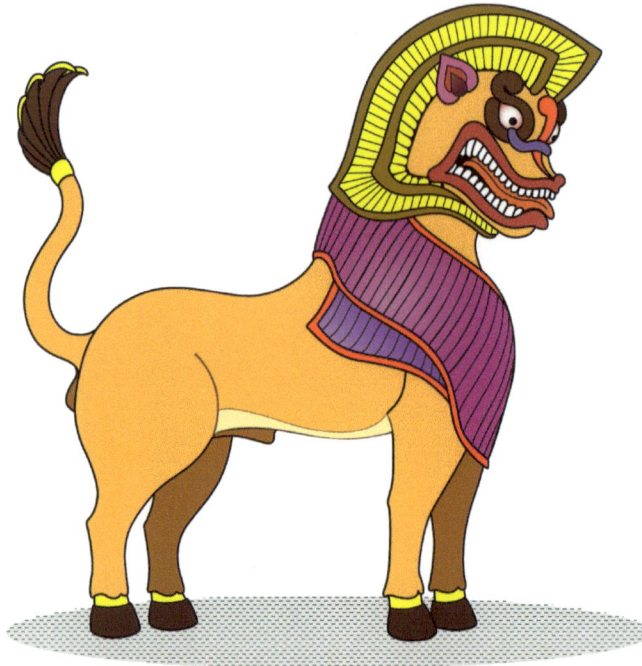

Strange animal. On door-jamb and pilaster, the Baphuon, Angkor Vat.

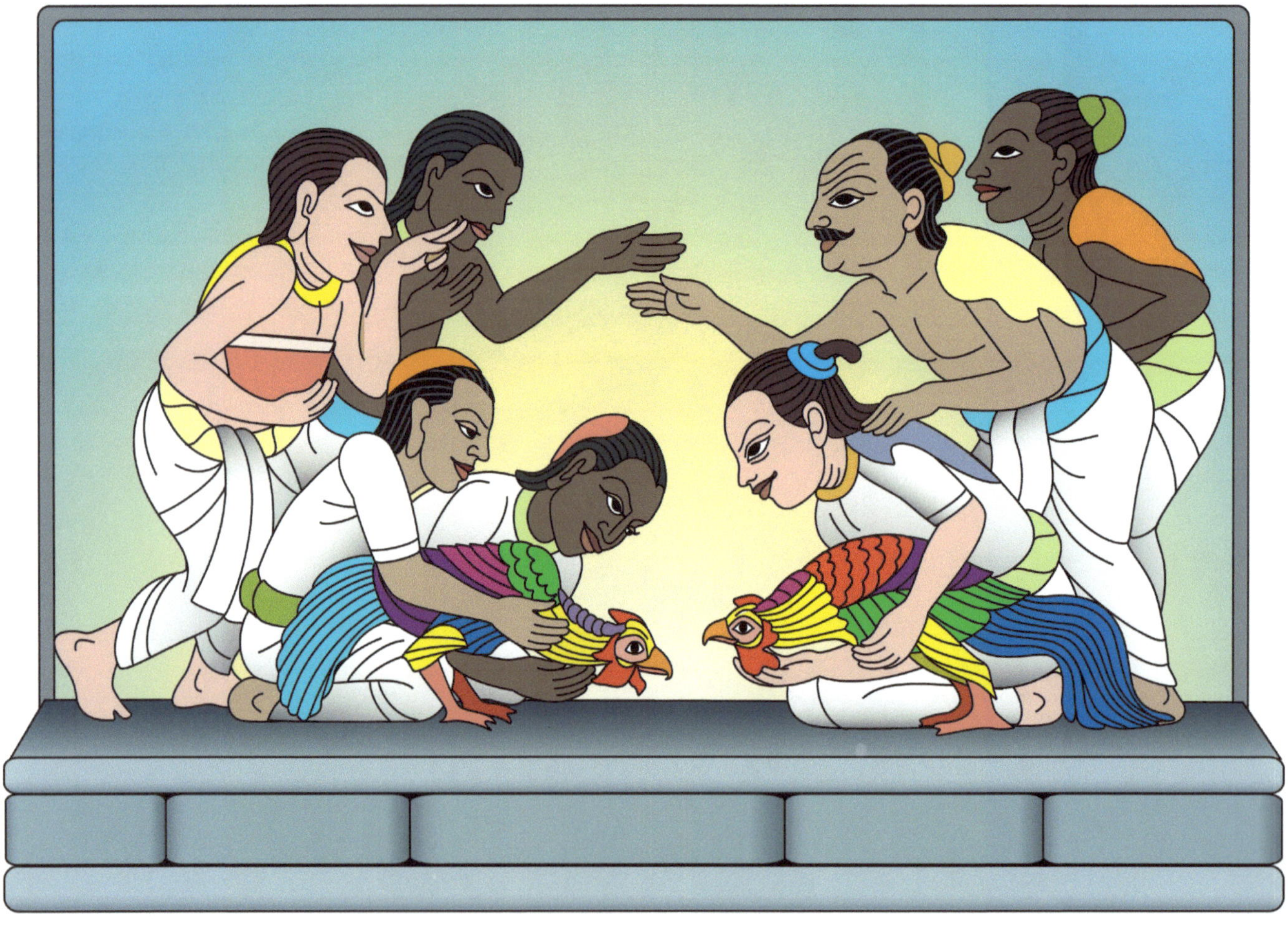

Bas-relief of a cockfight in the outer gallery of a temple at Angkor Thom. First half of the 13th Century C.E. The scene is marked by remarkable vivacity and the artist's ability to fit various figures into a limited space.

Cambodian Art

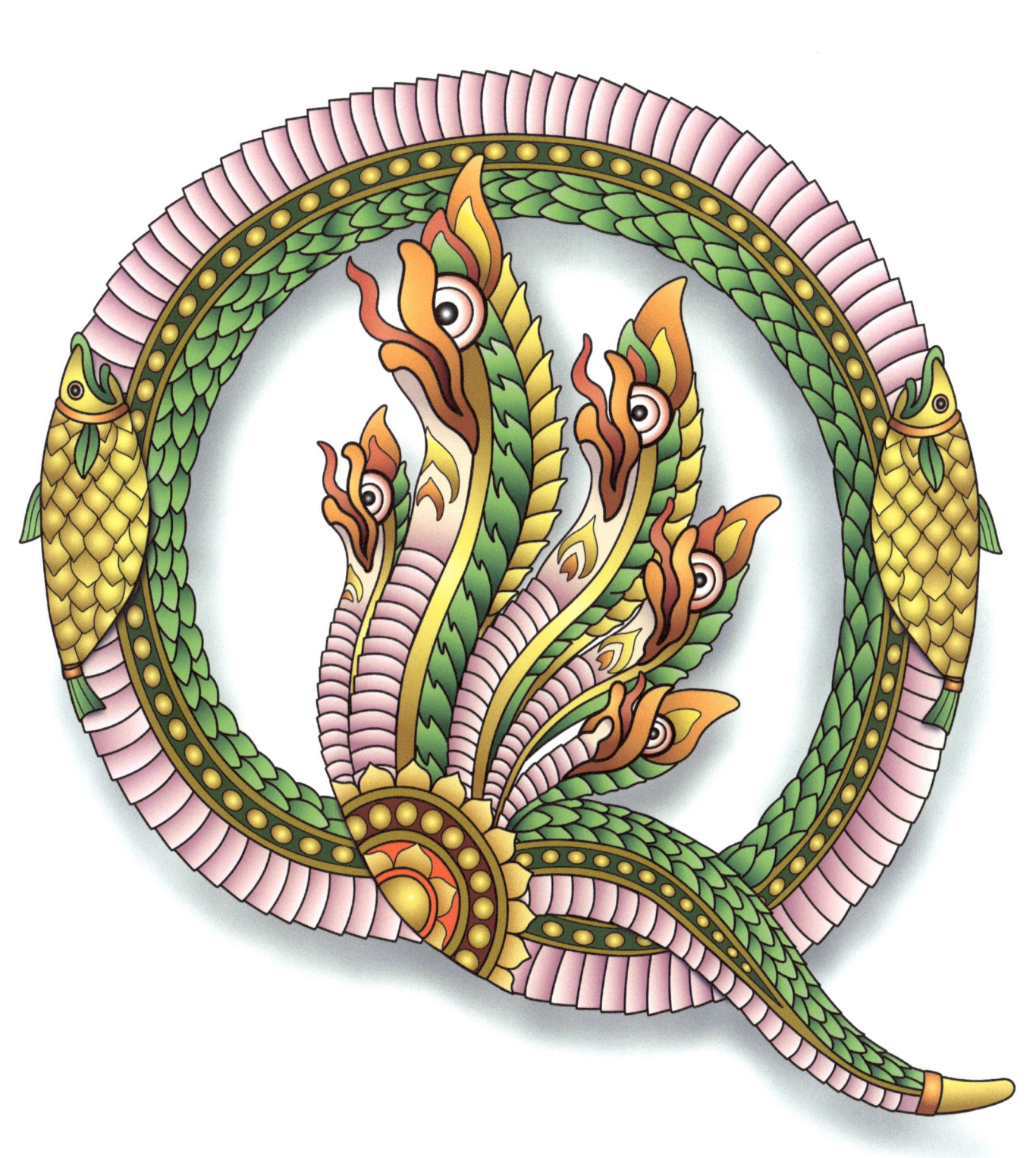

Bas-relief of the Snake god with five heads. Angkor Vat.

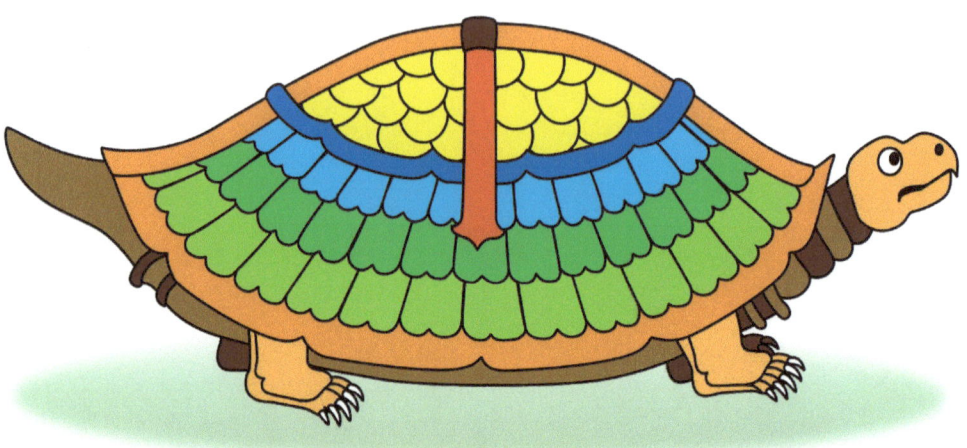

Kurma, the tortoise from a mythological scene in the relief work. The Bayon, Angkor Thom.

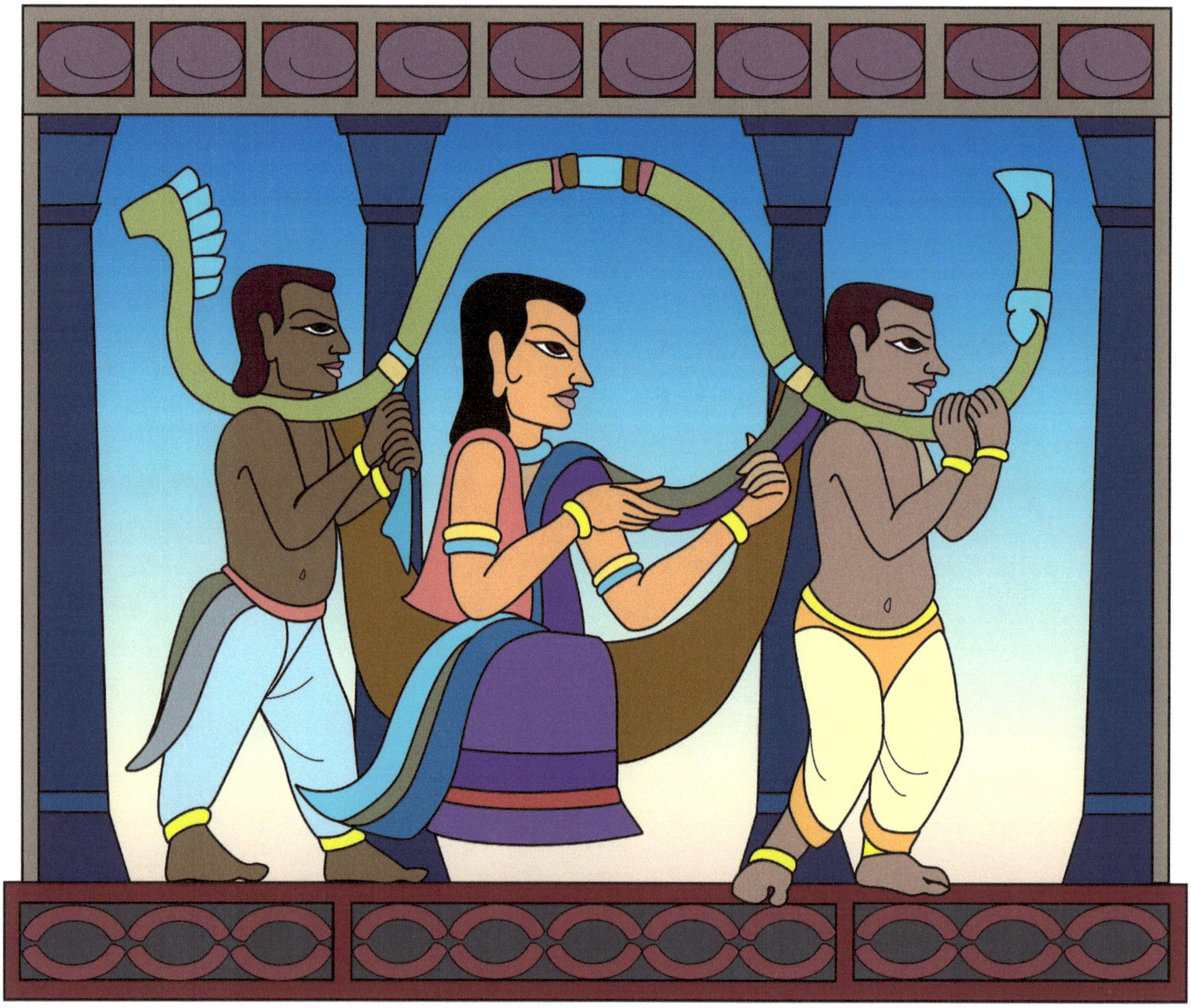

A relief showing one person is carried on a palanquin. The same type of palanquin was in use throughout Indo-Chinese up to the beginning of 20th Century C.E. The Bayon, Angkor Thom.

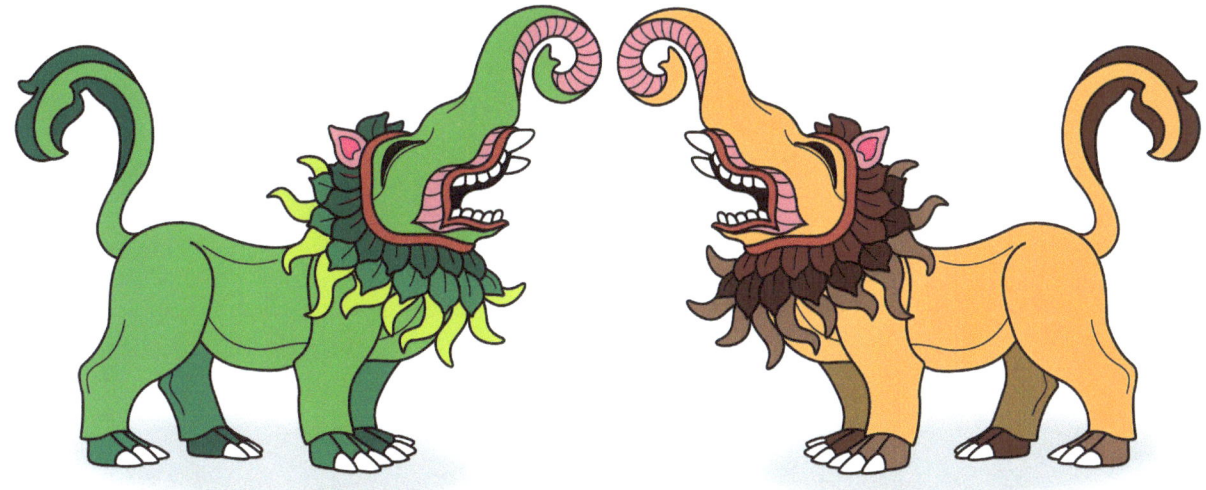

Probably Makara, a fabulous animal. Banteay Srei, Angkor Thom.

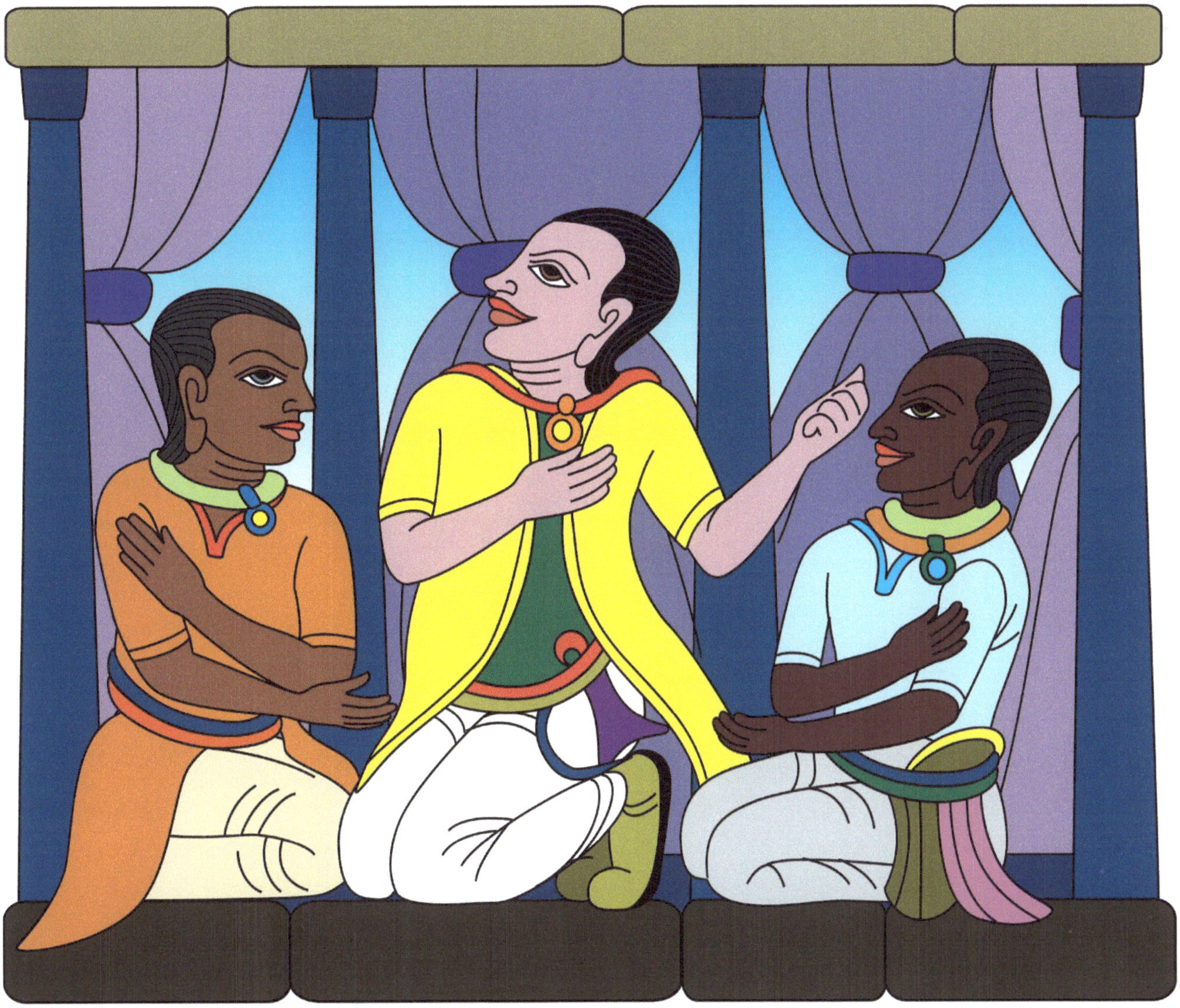

Bas-relief on the outer gallery. Representing the celebration of victory. The Bayon.

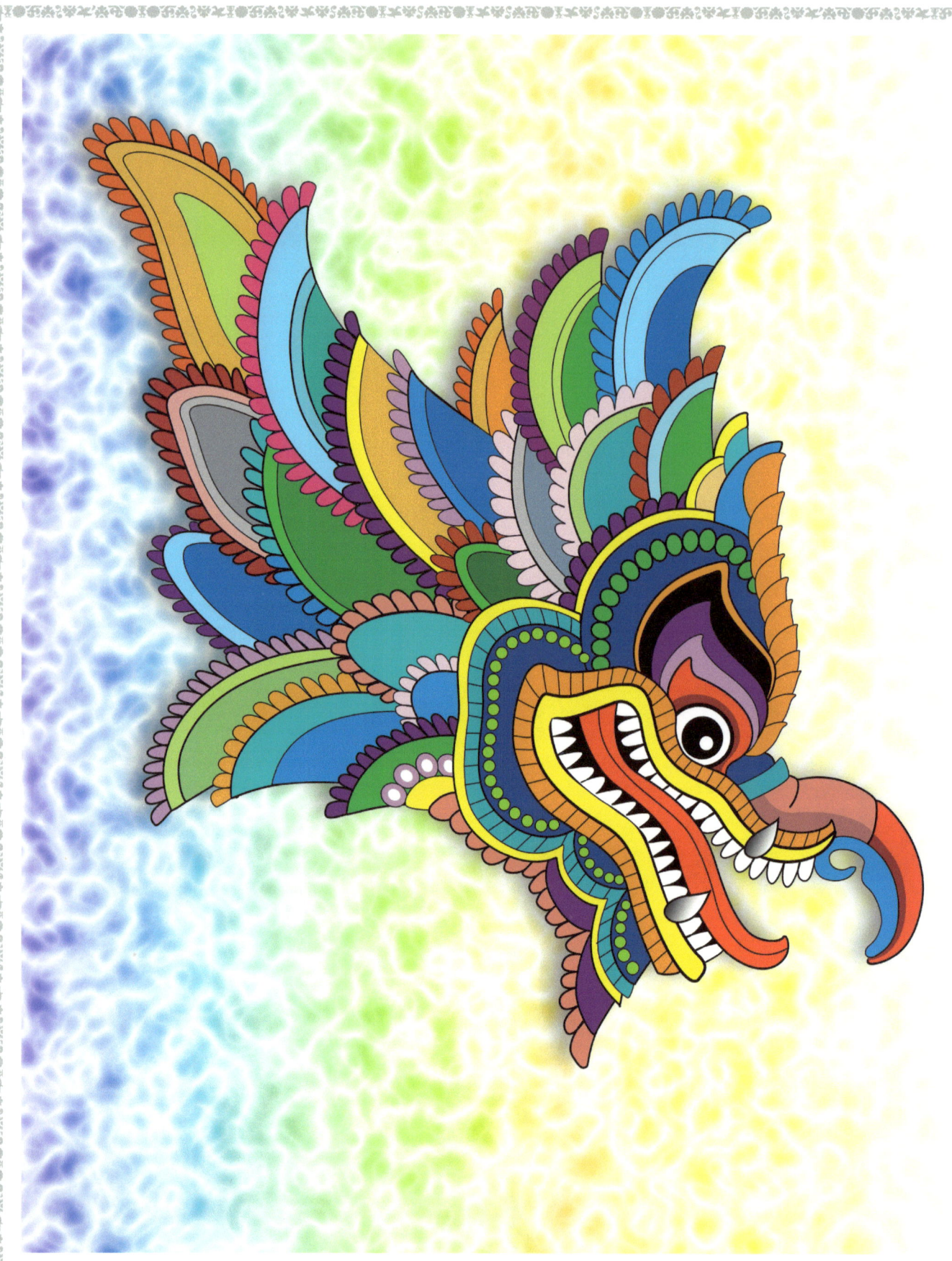

On a bas-relief, Angkor Wat. Head of a notorious
yet fantastic creature. Battle field, war of Lanka from the Ramayana.

Cambodian Art

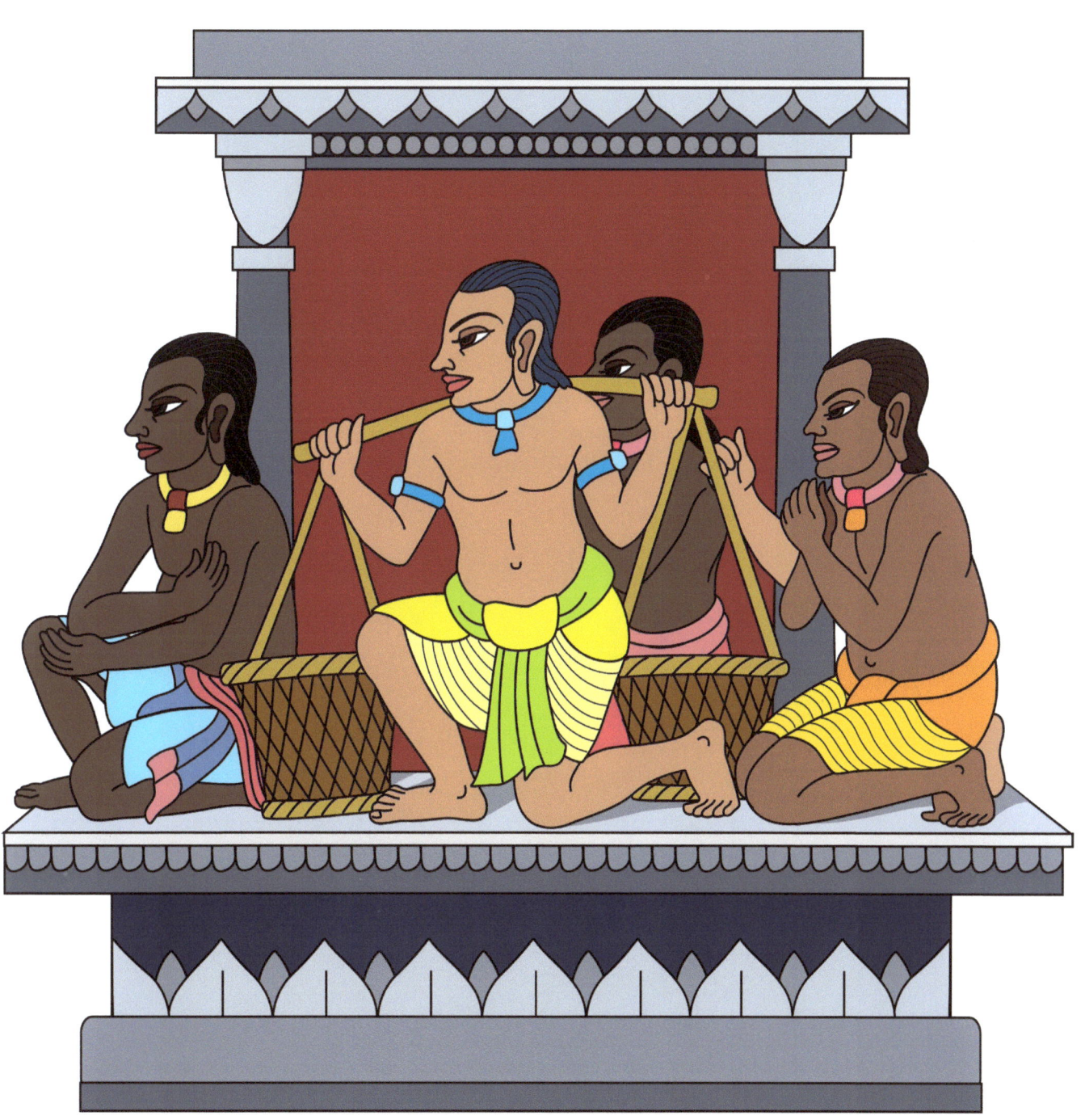

An episode from the daily life, on a bas-relief in the temple of the Bayon.

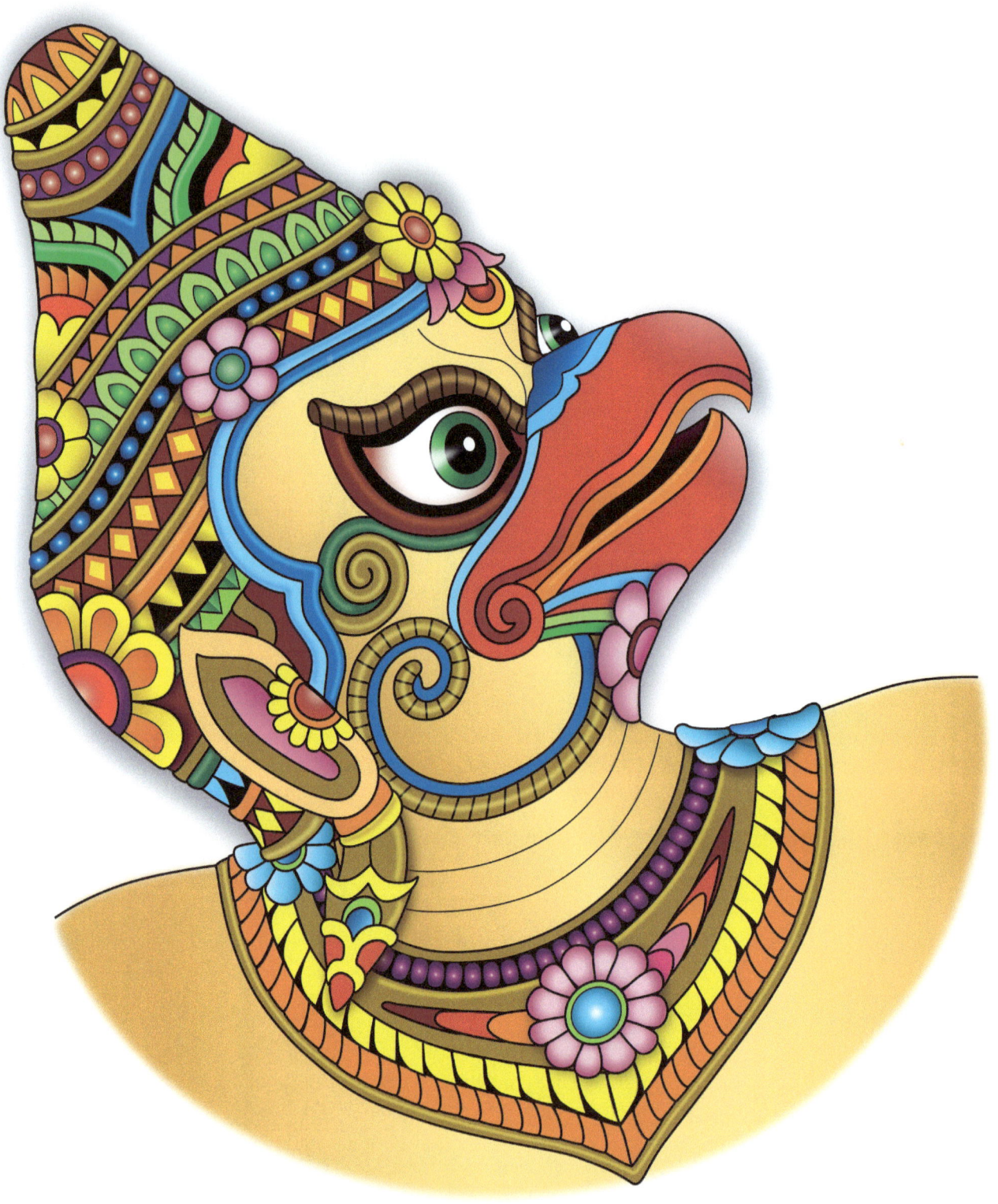

A Mythical character from the Battle of Lanka, bas-relief, Angkor Wat.
Figures and scenes are erected in different ways. Some are rigid, static, hierarchical;
others are done with freedom of movements that transmit a
dynamism to everything around them.

Cambodian Art

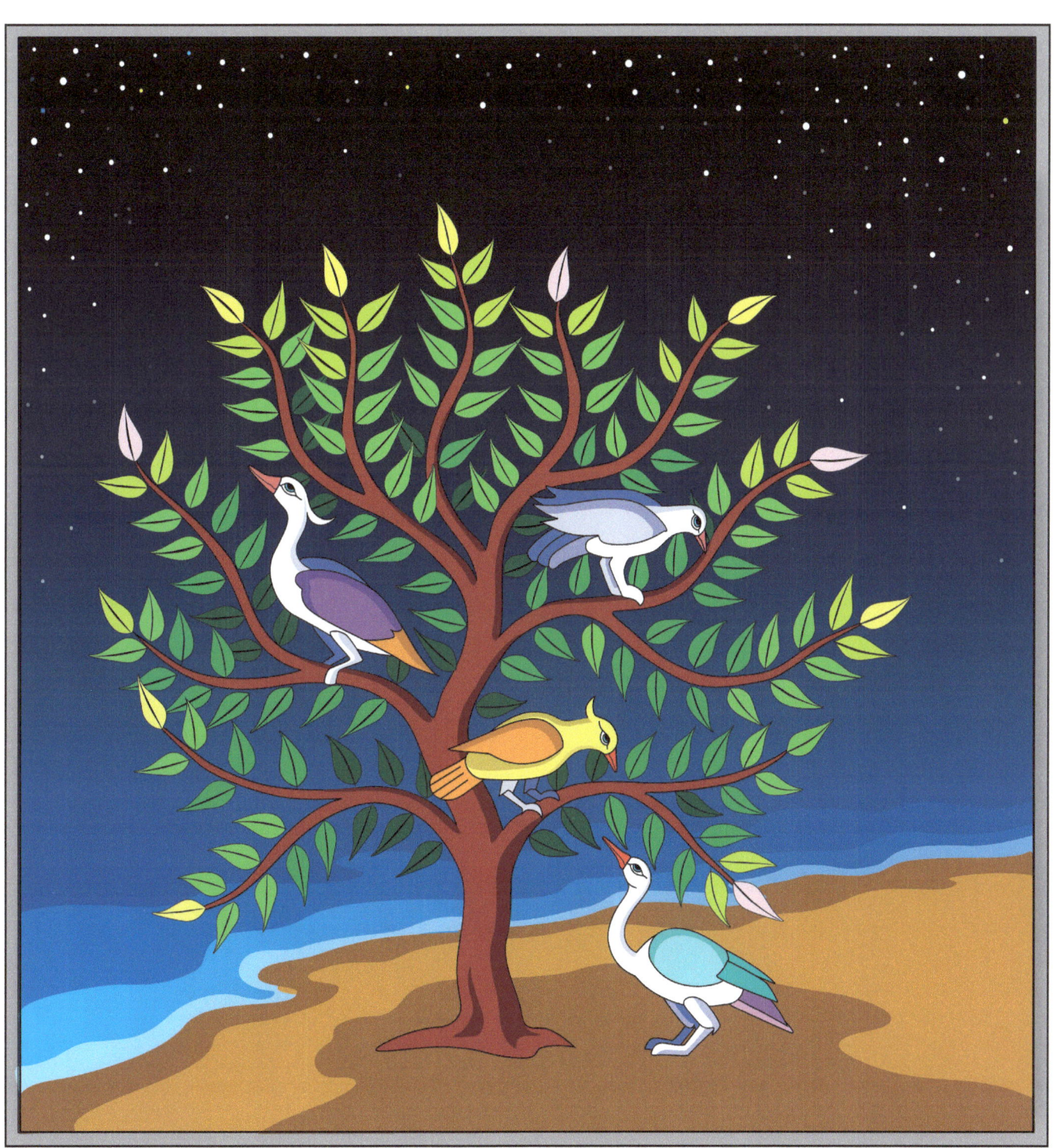

Beautiful birds, from bas-relief on the North 'library' at Banteay Srei, Angkor Wat.

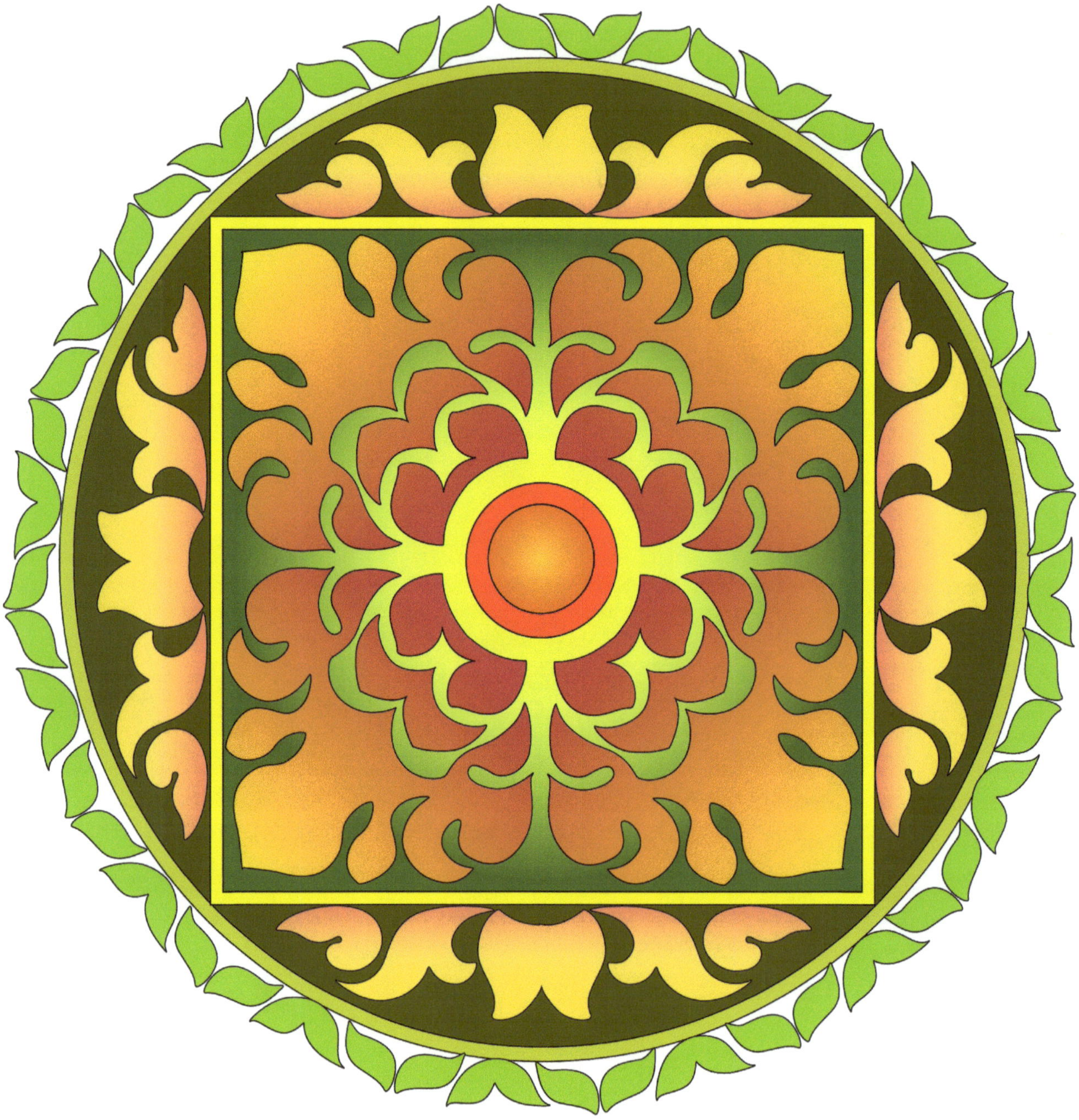

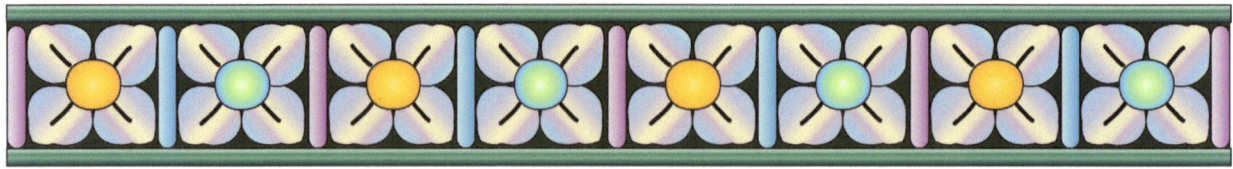

Examples of the images created using the elements found in Cambodian Art.

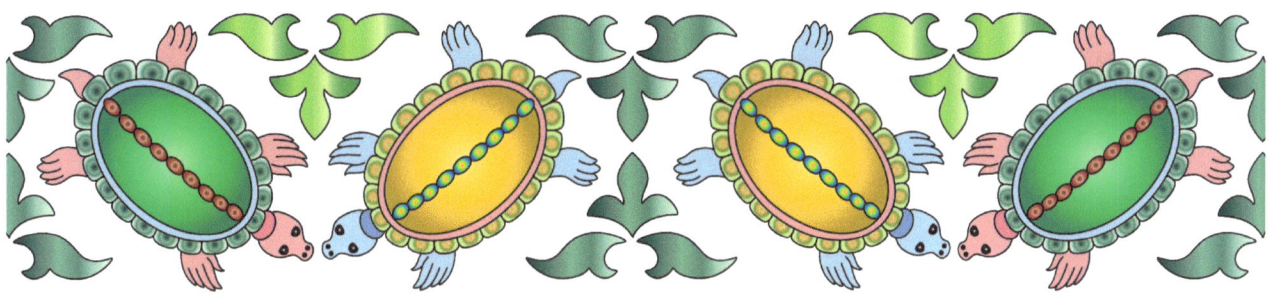

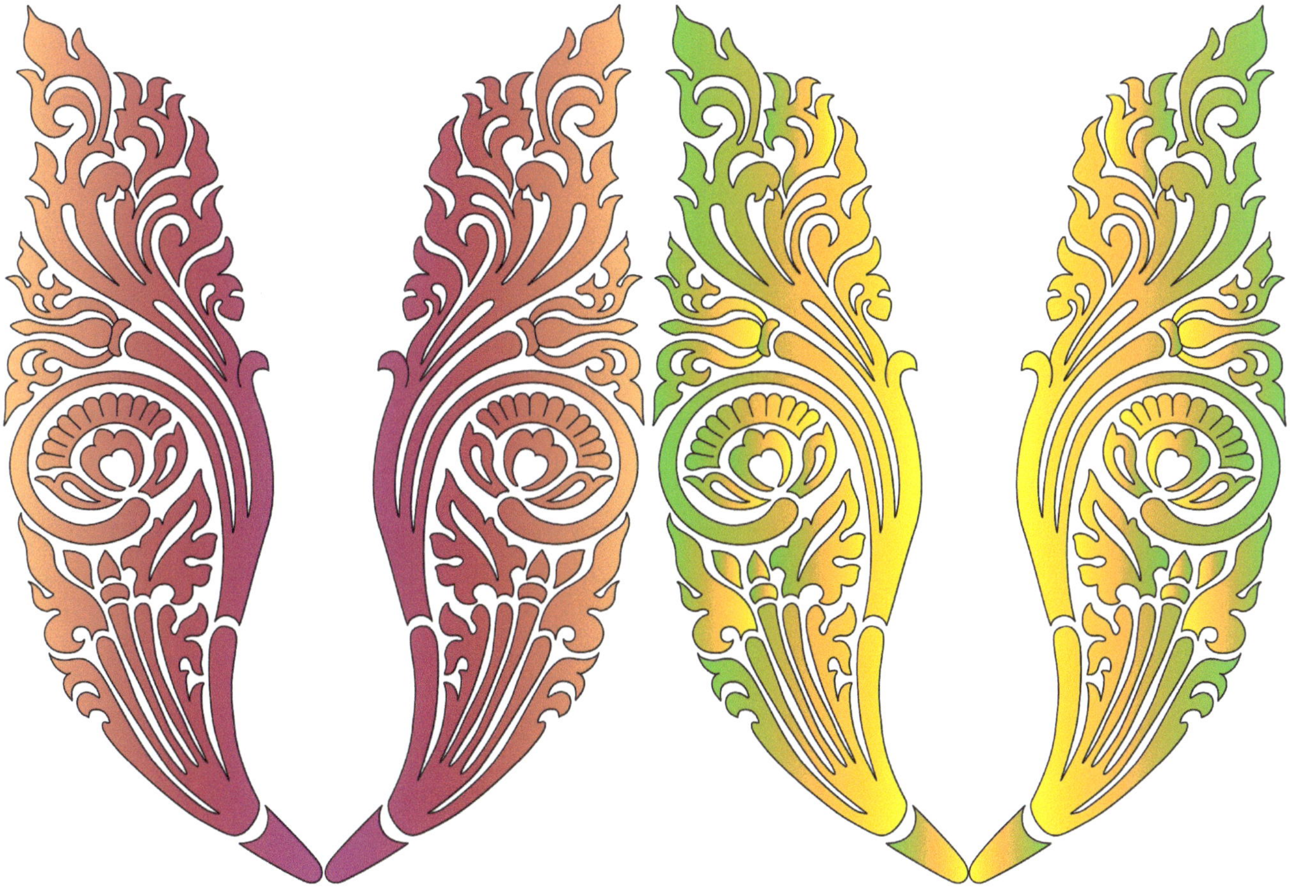

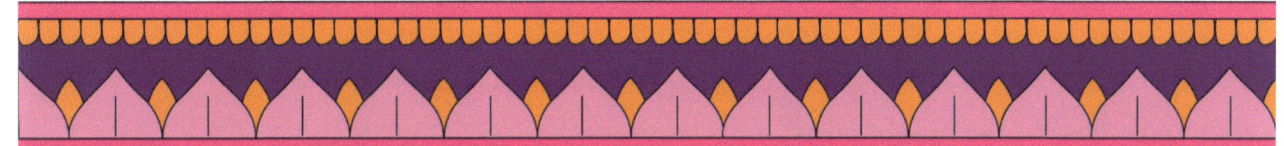

Examples of the images created using the elements found in Cambodian Art.

= a synopsis of =
indian art

Indian art is mostly visual art produced on the Indian subcontinent since 4000 B.C.E., and earlier. Indus Valley Civilization, also known as the Harappan Civilization had matured during 2600 - 1900 B.C.E. Sculptures made from stone, bronze, and clay in the Indus Valley Civilization had first introduced the distinct artistic elements that later became permanent characteristics of Indian art. Terracotta was the most treasured material for Indus sculptors.

The Stupas at Amravati, Sanchi, Bharhut, and others display the wealth of stone carvings. The themes that united the Stupas together are scenes from the life of Buddha. At the Sanchi Gates, there are depictions of warriors on horses, royal processions, traders, caravans, and merchants, farmers with produce and animals, and so forth. Indian temples sculpted images of musicians, acrobats, romantic couples, and a variety of deities. Hindu sculptures were naturalistic in all and mainly focused on creating humans, animals, vegetables, and other forms of life. Indian color, while sometimes shining with the lovely orange-amber light in the Ajanta cave paintings, is essentially delicate, and its use in decoration varies with each art.

Paintings in India have a very tradition with ancient texts outlining theories of color and aesthetics. Common households used to paint doorways and facades. Cave paintings from Ajanta, Bagh, and Sittanavasal, as well as temple paintings confirm the love of naturalizing the human form and nature in a manner that is aesthetically pleasing and as an embellishment. Miniature paintings on paper developed quickly in the late 16th Century from the combined influences of the existing Indian tradition and the imported Persian style by the Mughals. In many of the Indian Miniature paintings, emphasis is placed on mood or atmosphere through the bold use of color and deliberate flattering of three dimensional textures. The artists succeeded in bringing out hidden nuances that simply would not be possible any other way. In both the Mewer and in Kangra paintings, scenes of idyllic nature were created to convey joy and romance.

Folk and tribal art in India took on different manifestations through a varied media such as: pottery, painting, metal work, paper art, weaving, jewelry, toys and masks. All these play a great role in the populations both daily and ritual life. The folk spirit played an important part in the development of Indian art and in the overall perception of the indigenous people of India.

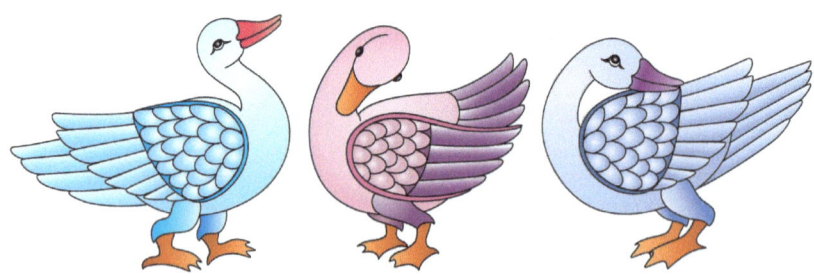

= a synopsis of =
Cambodian art

Khmer art reached its peak during the Angkor period, and between 900 and 1200 C.E., the Khmer Empire was some of world's most magnificent architectural beauty. The word Angkor derived from the Sanskrit word Nagar, which means city. The formidably enormous and incomparable monuments, the greatness along with beauty, and the vast wealth and strength of the Angkorian Civilization lasted some five centuries. Angkor was built especially for the divine powers of the Kings of Angkor.

Cambodian art stretches far back to the centuries old potteries, silk weaving, and stone carvings. Stone carving in Cambodia is the best known form of art. They adorned the temples in Angkor and are renowned for their scale, richness, and the fine details of the sculptures. Cambodia's lacquer-ware were at its prime between the 12th and 16th Century C.E. Lacquer-ware were by tradition colored black using burnt wood to represent the underworld, red using mercury which symbolized the earth and yellow using arsenic to signify the heavens.

King Suryavarman II, who reigned over the Khmer Empire during 1113 - 1150 C.E., built the Angkor temples. Angkor Wat was the largest and the most harmonious of all the temples during that time. It was built within the period of 37 years and was solely dedicated to the God Vishnu. The temple represents the prodigious funeral pyre of a divine king, with its many towers, courtyards, and scenes from the great Indian epics, the Ramayana and the Mahabharata. In the Banteay Srei district, The Citadel of Women is the most popular and the style is even similar to the Indian style.

Years later, King Jayavarman VII, built the Bayon temple, which was his greatest undertaking in the centre of Angkor Thom. It is known to be the most extraordinary and yet strange monument in the world. The enormous sculpture is of a lotus with four faces, and eight eyes, multiplied by all the flowers appearing to envelop the whole world. They carved their lives, their laughter, their death, alongside the great friezes of the wars and triumphs with their warriors in chariots, and nobles in palanquins. They also carved various events from their domestic lives.

Unfortunately, later in the years, the Angkor Wat was left abandoned as the capital city of Khmers when the invaders settled in. Only in the early 20th Century was the city restored when a French explorer rediscovered it.

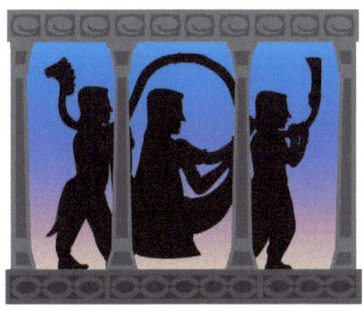

OTHER TITLES IN THIS SERIES

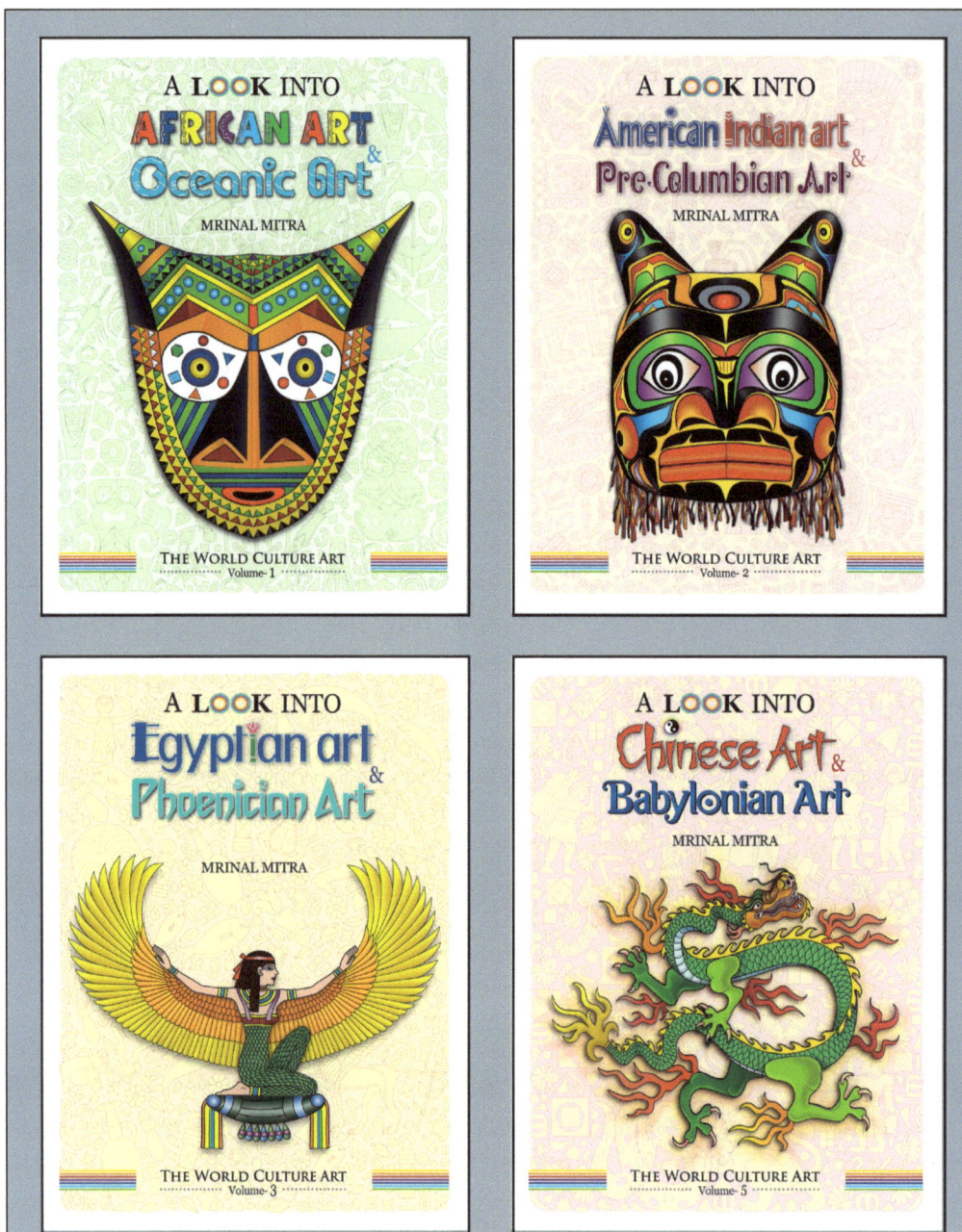

About the Author

Mrinal Mitra has earned a number of prestigious awards, both Indian and International, and received honors for his outstanding illustrations. Some of his recognitions include; The Noma Concours Award (twice), Tokyo, Japan, Illustrators Award, and Children`s Choice Award, India, and Honors from German Television `Transtel`, BRNO- CSSR, TIBI- Iran, and UNICEF, New York, USA.

Many of his talented artworks have been exhibited in various countries such as; India, Japan, Italy, Czech Republic, Iran, and New Zealand. Mitra has authored, designed, and illustrated trades and educational children books for many Indian as well as Multinational Book Publishers around the globe.

Copyright: Mrinal Mitra, 2016

All rights reserved. No part of this book may be reproduced in any form without permission in writing from the Author or Publisher.

Printed by CreateSpace, an Amazom.com company.
Available from Amazon.com, CreateSpace.com, and other retail outlets.

www.ingramcontent.com/pod-product-compliance
Lightning Source LLC
Chambersburg PA
CBHW040419220526
45473CB00004B/1294